"*Small Groups Made Easy* d
leading a small group easy. Th
concise, and applicable. They
And the studies answer some of the mo~~~
ling questions both new and longtime believers ask."

Larry Osborne, pastor, North Coast Church;
author, *Lead Like a Shepherd*

"In *Small Groups Made Easy*, Ryan not only lays out the biblical foundation for groups and group leadership, but also provides a road map for new leaders to follow. Once a new small group is launched, the included twelve Bible studies will help assure they are headed in the right direction spiritually."

Chris Surratt, small group and discipleship specialist,
LifeWay Christian Resources; author, *Leading Small Groups*
and *Small Groups for the Rest of Us*

"Ryan Lokkesmoe takes complex topics and boils them down to chewable bites, easily digested by laypeople. In *Small Groups Made Easy*, Lokkesmoe addresses typical frustrations of group leaders, then provides studies on foundational topics that most everyone wrestles with. He doesn't tell us what to think but rather how to think and then discuss as a group. With its accessible title, clear explanations, and relevant content, *Small Groups Made Easy* will be a valuable resource for our leaders."

Michelle Attar, pastor of adult ministries,
Bent Tree Bible Fellowship

"In this book, Ryan does a great job of addressing something that has not been written about previously—preparing yourself to lead a small group. This is a must-have for any small group pastor or point person to draw from as they formulate how they are going to equip their leaders."

Brian Brunke, small group operations pastor,
Parkway Fellowship; small group network regional leader
(Texas, Oklahoma, Arkansas, Louisiana),
The Small Group Network

"*Small Groups Made Easy* by Ryan Lokkesmoe is a wonderful resource for small group leaders. In addition to practical advice, it offers twelve great small group studies on topics ranging from prayer to spiritual growth, from finances to broken relationships. This book will be a huge help to anyone leading or thinking about leading a small group."

Steve Gladen, pastor of small groups, Saddleback Church; author, *Leading Small Groups with Purpose*

"If you've been digging for a book that is both practical and theological, this is the unfound treasure you've been seeking. *Small Groups Made Easy* answers the theological questions group members are asking while being a down-to-earth guidebook to small group leadership. Every small group leader needs a copy of this in their library!"

Rick Howerton, church consultant, Kentucky Baptist Convention; founding pastor, The Bridge Church, Spring Hill, Tennessee

"*Small Groups Made Easy* is the resource for every pastor who knows the value of small groups but needs a starting point! As a senior pastor, I tend to overthink small groups, which makes me fearful or hesitant to move forward in implementation. Ryan Lokkesmoe masterfully provides a plan to move your church forward right now. We are eager to use this resource to equip our leaders and engage our groups at Emmanuel. I love Ryan's heart for the gospel and for local church ministry!"

Cary Schmidt, senior pastor, Emmanuel Baptist Church, Newington, Connecticut

SMALL GROUPS MADE EASY

SMALL GROUPS MADE EASY

**Practical and Biblical Starting Points
to Lead Your Gathering**

RYAN LOKKESMOE

BETHANYHOUSE

a division of Baker Publishing Group
Minneapolis, Minnesota

© 2019 by Ryan Lokkesmoe

Published by Bethany House Publishers
11400 Hampshire Avenue South
Bloomington, Minnesota 55438
www.bethanyhouse.com

Bethany House Publishers is a division of
Baker Publishing Group, Grand Rapids, Michigan

Printed in the United States of America

Library of Congress Cataloging-in-Publication Data
Names: Lokkesmoe, Ryan, author.
Title: Small groups made easy : practical and biblical starting points to
lead your gathering / Ryan Lokkesmoe.
Description: Minneapolis, Minnesota : Bethany House Publishers, [2019] | Includes
bibliographic references.
Identifiers: LCCN 2019021183 | ISBN 9780764233913 (trade paperback) | ISBN
9781493421794 (ebook)
Subjects: LCSH: Church group work. | Small groups—Religious aspects—
Christianity. | Christian leadership. | Bible—Outlines, syllabi, etc.
Classification: LCC BV652.2 .L65 2019 | DDC 253/.7—dc23
LC record available at https://lccn.loc.gov/2019021183

Cover design by Dan Pitts

Author represented by Books & Such Literary Agency

19 20 21 22 23 24 25   7 6 5 4 3 2 1

Contents

1

Classic Christianity

Despite having a rather generic name, small groups are vibrant and diverse. Some meet in the morning at coffee shops, others in the evening at church buildings. Some gather in public spaces like parks or libraries. Some have three members; others have thirty. Some small groups are part of large-scale church ministries with standardized curriculum. Others are little gatherings of friends, family, or neighbors. Some groups are focused on studying Scripture; others are more relationally driven, organized around a shared interest or activity. Some gather sporadically, others like clockwork every week. You will find small groups studying the Bible in the break rooms of upscale corporate offices, and you will find them praying for each other in shacks without running water.

Regardless of their size, location, or focus, a small gathering of Christians is the most ancient ministry practice of the Church. This is classic Christianity, born in an era before there were such things as large church buildings. In the earliest days of the Church, women and men of faith would gather together wherever they could: the homes of church members, cramped apartments, the marketplace, lecture halls, and even catacombs.[1] In the words of biblical scholar Graydon Snyder, "The New Testament Church began as a small group house church (Col. 4:15) and it remained so until the middle or end of the third century. There are no evidences of larger places of meeting before [the year] 300."[2] The first-century Christians would have been stunned to see the prominent church buildings that have become so commonplace in our modern world.

The early Christians did not choose small groups as a strategy among carefully weighed options; it was simply the way of the first-century Mediterranean world. There were relatively few Christians and no dedicated church buildings. The Holy Spirit, however, does not require large crowds and construction projects to do his work and grow the Church. The Spirit moved powerfully through the simple model of small gatherings. Friendships were forged. Scripture was studied. Prayers were prayed. The gospel was shared. People took care of each other. The same is true today of Christian small groups. This is true in wealthy communities that have the luxury of viewing small groups as a ministry strategy, and this is true in places where small groups are the only option due to poverty, persecution, or scarcity of Christians.

If you choose to lead a small group today, you have stepped onto a well-worn path, a time-honored tradition of the Church. You are following in the footsteps of millions of Christians who have led gatherings in their homes and communities. God

1. Acts 19:9; Romans 16:5; 1 Corinthians 16:19; Colossians 4:15; Philemon 1:2; see also Robert Jewett, "Tenement Churches and Pauline Love Feasts," *Quarterly Review* 14, no. 1 (1994): 43–58.
2. Graydon F. Snyder, *Ante-Pacem: Archaeological Evidence of Church Life Before Constantine* (Macon, GA: Mercer University Press, 2003), 299.

worked powerfully through them, and you can rest assured that he will work through you as well.

Over the years, I've led and participated in many small groups. I've been a part of several churches in different cities with a variety of philosophies on groups. I had the privilege of serving as a small-groups pastor at a large, rapidly growing church that went from a single campus to multisite during my time on staff. I've attended large and small conferences on groups, taught by experts in small-group ministry. I've read most of what's out there on how to effectively shepherd a small-group ministry, and as a pastor I've experienced both successes and failures in implementing the rich wisdom that was shared with me.

But this is not a book about how to design and run a small-group system. There are plenty of excellent books out there on that important subject. I hope, instead, to focus on the human and spiritual aspects of leading a group.

A key problem with small groups today is that despite a wealth of literature and training opportunities, many group leaders doubt they are up to the task. When facing the very normal challenges that occur in most groups, leaders wonder if those challenges are evidence that they're not cut out to lead—proof that their apprehensions are justified. I have felt those concerns myself as I have led groups, and I have worked with many gifted leaders who express the same anxieties. It's very common to wonder those things, because there are aspects of group leadership that defy even the best training and systems, things like spiritual leadership and human relationships. There is no one-size-fits-all approach for leadership in these areas, so it's important to accept that these types of challenges will come to you; don't be surprised or rattled by them.

A small group should be effective and enjoyable. Both of those dimensions are important. If a group is *enjoyable* but does not disciple its members or foster friendships, then it may not be particularly effective. On the other hand, a group might be *effective* at nurturing spiritual growth at the cost of your enjoyment as the leader. If this is the case, you will exhaust yourself, and the group's effectiveness will inevitably suffer.

As the subtitle of this book states, my aim is to give you some starting points that will help you lead a group that flourishes over time and *feels* easy. For that to be possible, some expectations must be managed. Challenges must be normalized. And you should be prepared to lead both pragmatically and biblically. Offering practical leadership guidance without some foundational theological preparation is—in my opinion—a highly impractical thing to do, because as any seasoned small-group leader will tell you, many of the challenges that face small groups have to do with spiritual concerns—not logistical ones.

I will not spend time in this book weighing the merits of various small-group ministry strategies. Put another way, I'm going to be less focused on big-S Small Groups, i.e., modern, narrowly defined ministry systems typically practiced in large churches. I will instead speak to the larger category of little-s small groups, i.e., gatherings of Christians that happen to be small.[3]

If your group is part of a large-scale church ministry, I'm going to assume that you've been given some training by your pastor about the purpose of your group and how it fits into your church's broader strategy to achieve discipleship and community. My hope is that this book will not compete with any other resources you've been given, but will instead complement and reinforce what you've already learned. If you've been given no preparation, this book will be a good starting point.

3. My distinction between big-S Small Groups and little-s small groups is inspired by Tim Keller's differentiation between big-E Evangelicalism and little-e evangelicalism.

Here is how we will proceed. The next four chapters (part 1) will focus on some simple, practical principles for leading your group well. After that (part 2), I have written twelve starter Bible studies designed to do two things:

1. Prepare you to address important biblical questions that often arise in small-group discussions
2. Model how to approach your group meetings

Each of the twelve studies will also help you gain a sense of how to ask the right types of questions—questions about your group members' lives and questions about the topic being studied. Asking the right questions—not having all the answers—will set the stage for growing friendships and a deeper engagement with God's Word.

These twelve starter studies in part 2 can be used as either your own personal devotional to prepare you for leading your group, or they can be used as twelve weeks of study material for your group to go through together. I leave that up to you.

Before we continue, a brief word of encouragement is in order. Leading a small group is a biblical, God-honoring thing to do. That does not mean it will be challenge-free. Keep a watch on your expectations. Don't regard quick, observable life change as the singular measure of success. Don't expect that all of your group members will become lifelong friends. Over time, you will see lives changed, and you will see friendships grow, but transformation takes time and it's God's business. Remember two things as you embark on leading a group:

1. **Rely on the Lord.** As Jesus said in John 15:5: "I am the vine; you are the branches. If you remain in me and I in you, you will bear much fruit; apart from me you can

do nothing." Leading your group well is not all on your shoulders. Focus on your own relationship with Jesus, and ask him to supernaturally enable you to lead well in his name. You are not meant to bear the full burden of leadership on your own.

2. **Just keep meeting.** You will experience ups and downs in your group. There will be times that are encouraging and other times that are less so. There will be seasons when your group meets very consistently with little effort, and times when it's difficult to get your schedules lined up. Just keep gathering. As the writer of Hebrews put it: "Let us consider how we may spur one another on toward love and good deeds, not giving up meeting together, as some are in the habit of doing, but encouraging one another" (Hebrews 10:24–25).

My hope is that after reading this book, you will feel prepared to lead, both biblically and practically. It is my prayer that leading a small group would be an enjoyable, life-giving experience for you, and that it would *feel* easy even when—especially when—life isn't easy.

PART ONE

PRACTICAL STARTING POINTS

2

Clarifying Your Role

One of the toughest things to do in any leadership role is to quiet that second voice—our inner commentator that talks to us in real time as we attempt to speak publicly or lead others. The volume of this voice seems to increase in direct proportion to our insecurity, and it rarely (if ever) encourages us. Listening to our inner pundit amplifies the challenges inherent to leadership.

In my experience, the voice chimes in when I attempt to assess how people are responding to what I'm saying. If I'm speaking in front of a crowd, the second voice kicks in when I'm not getting much nonverbal feedback or when someone makes a confused face, seems distracted, or leaves the room. When leading small groups, my inner analyst speaks up when the group is quiet—during those awkward silences after I've asked a question.

Are they getting anything out of this group? I think to myself. *Do I seem prepared? Am I being transparent enough? Why does everyone seem so tired? Why am I so tired?* These are the kinds of thoughts that creep in, and while they can be disheartening in the moment, they're actually very typical thoughts for anyone who endeavors to lead.

One of the reasons we find these inner narratives so compelling is that whether we realize it or not, we have in our minds a picture of what the ideal leader looks and sounds like. Sometimes the ideal pattern is based on a hero or mentor of ours that we can't imagine living up to. If we're leading a staff meeting, we have an idea of what a good leader looks like in that context. If we're coaching a team, there's a paradigm in our minds of what an excellent coach acts like. If we're leading a small group, we have some notion of how it should be going. Often we're unaware that we are measuring ourselves against this ideal pattern. The comparison is just happening in the background.

How does this play out in the context of leading small groups? We find ourselves thinking that we need to be a biblical scholar. A seasoned pastor. A professional counselor. A real-time theologian. In some cases, a world-class chef or barista. We feel pressure to be the smartest person in the room or have all the answers. If we don't—the inner logic goes—then why are we leading?

We will limp through small-group leadership if we don't counteract this thinking with the truth of Scripture: what God told us about ourselves, about each other, and about what it means to lead in Jesus's name. Also, we must never forget that Satan—the accuser and tireless cynic—wants you to think that you're not up to the task of leading. He wants you to effortlessly remember your flaws and dwell on your supposed shortcomings. Don't be surprised when he lies to you about your group and your leadership.

Let's now walk through a few New Testament passages that will provide truth and encouragement as you think about leading a small group.

Leadership according to Jesus

When Jesus saw his disciples getting caught up in a leadership mindset that was competitive and achievement oriented, he countered their thinking by letting them know that his vision of leadership was fundamentally different. He contrasted the authoritarian leadership style of the Roman authorities with the kind of leadership outlook he wanted his followers to embrace. In the gospel of Matthew we read,

> Jesus called them together and said, "You know that the rulers of the Gentiles lord it over them, and their high officials exercise authority over them. Not so with you. Instead, whoever wants to become great among you must be your servant, and whoever wants to be first must be your slave—just as the Son of Man did not come to be served, but to serve, and to give his life as a ransom for many."
>
> Matthew 20:25–28

The rulers of the Gentiles—the Roman imperial administration—rooted their leadership in honor, authority, achievement, and respect. Just before this passage in Matthew, the mother of James and John had asked Jesus if her two sons could enjoy special seats of honor in his kingdom. When the other disciples got wind of this, they were indignant about it. They were all viewing leadership from a very worldly, success-driven perspective. But Jesus clearly stated that it will not be that way with those who wish to lead in his name. It's not about being the best or better than others. Whoever wants to be great will be a servant. Whoever wants to be first must think of themselves as a slave, i.e., someone who represents not the top rung on society's ladder, but the very bottom—the social opposite of Caesar.

And Jesus meant it, because he himself embodied this perspective. He took on flesh not to come and be served—which of course he was entitled to do—but to serve. This is the attitude that we are meant to have as followers of Christ, and certainly as those who would lead others in his name. The apostle Paul reinforced this point in his letter to the Philippians, writing that we should have the same mindset as Christ,

> who, being in very nature God, did not consider equality with God something to be used to his own advantage; rather, he made himself nothing by taking the very nature of a servant, being made in human likeness. And being found in appearance as a man, he humbled himself by becoming obedient to death.

> Philippians 2:6–8

Once we are clued into Jesus's countercultural paradigm of leadership, we begin to see this humble, others-oriented posture showing up throughout the rest of the New Testament. For example, Paul wrote to the Roman Christians, "I long to see you so that I may impart to you some spiritual gift to make you strong—that is, that you and I may be mutually encouraged by each other's faith" (Romans 1:11–12).

Paul doesn't view himself as a teacher with nothing to learn from those he is leading; he desires to be encouraged by the Roman believers even as he is encouraging them. Paul was communicating to them (and us) that he didn't view himself as necessary for the entirety of their spiritual growth. In fact, he later adds in the same letter: "I myself am convinced, my brothers and sisters, that you yourselves are full of goodness, filled with knowledge and competent to instruct one another" (Romans 15:14).

Paul trusted that God would work through the Roman Christians to help one another grow, and that the growth they experienced wouldn't be dependent on Paul's presence. He paints a similar picture in his letter to the Colossians: "Let the message of Christ dwell among you richly as you teach and admonish one another with all wisdom through psalms, hymns, and songs from the Spirit, singing to God with gratitude in your hearts" (Colossians 3:16).

What Does This Mean for Small-Group Leadership?

The antidote to that inner critic isn't about trying harder, learning more, or being better. It's about asking Jesus to replace your earthly definitions of leadership with his. There is no "right" type of leader. Leading others in a small group is not about your competence or knowledge or proving your worth. It's about serving and relying on Jesus to do his work through you. You are not meant to be a biblical scholar, theologian, or professional counselor. You are not meant to view yourself as indispensable to your group. Your goal is to be a servant of your group members, trusting that God will work through your leadership to achieve his purposes, and that he will work through your group members to encourage *you*. Be their friend, a facilitator of meaningful conversations, and an example to your group— not a model of perfection, but an example of someone who is faithfully following Christ and trusting him through the ups and downs of life.

As you faithfully lead, you will discover that your group members are growing in their relationship with the Lord, and in their relationships with each other. It may not happen at an even pace or in a predictable manner, but over time you will begin to see things as Paul saw them when he wrote to the Thessalonian Christians: "We ought always to thank God for you, brothers and sisters, and rightly so, because your faith is growing more and more, and the love all of you have for one another is increasing" (2 Thessalonians 1:3).

3

Logistical Matters

Architects, engineers, and city planners do not go about their business hoping that things won't go wrong; they plan for things to go awry, and design their cities and structures to be durable in the face of a variety of challenges.

After a devastating hurricane in 1900, the city of Galveston, Texas, took decisive action to prevent another catastrophe, building a seventeen-foot seawall and painstakingly raising the level of over two thousand city structures.[1] When architects design buildings in flood- or earthquake-prone areas, their plans must account for the natural risks. When skyscrapers and bridges are built, engineers design them to be able to flex as a response to the strains brought on by weather and other geological stresses. The same is true for airplane wings—they are built to remain strong even as they bend.

The point is this: It is wise to know the challenges that will probably arise with any endeavor, and to preemptively manage

1. Erik Larson, *Isaac's Storm: A Man, a Time, and the Deadliest Hurricane in History* (New York: Vintage Books, 2000), 265.

both the problems themselves and your expectations about them. The next few chapters will attempt to address the normal challenges that most small groups face. In my experience, if leaders' expectations are out of alignment, they will struggle more than necessary when logistical, personal, and spiritual challenges inevitably present themselves. In many cases, I've seen leaders respond to routine problems as if they're unusual—as signs that the leader isn't up for the task. That is simply not the case.

I will attempt in this chapter to prepare you for the problems inherent to small-group leadership, ordinary problems that tend to fall into these categories: attendance, communication, leadership, location, and childcare.

Attendance

A small group that endures over time will not have perfect attendance as its goal. No small group will ever have perfect attendance, and holding yourself as a leader to that standard—or anything close to perfect attendance—is an unrealistic expectation that will only discourage you. There are, however, two factors to focus on that will keep your attendance expectations healthy and set you up for quality gatherings: (1) critical mass and (2) the right frequency of meetings.

Critical mass is the minimum number of people you need to have a successful group meeting—a baseline attendance level you'd like to see more often than not. This number is different depending on the unique culture of each group. For a large group of twenty to thirty people, having only eight people at a gathering might feel discouraging or make the conversations a tad awkward. Critical mass for that group might be around fifteen people.

For other groups, three people at a meeting would be just fine because that group prefers a deeper relational connection and a certain level of confidentiality. So if there were six or seven people in that group and only three showed up to a particular meeting, it wouldn't be discouraging or awkward. In fact, that group might prefer to have only three or so show up.

Each group is unique, and you as the leader need to have a ballpark sense of what minimum number you'd like to see at most of your meetings. It's possible you won't be able to tell what critical mass looks like for your group until you've experienced a meeting that didn't go so well because too few people showed up. If that happens, don't be discouraged; just view it as an opportunity to sharpen your understanding of your group's critical mass number.

The second thing to focus on—which relates to critical mass—is the right frequency of meetings. If you meet too often, you might find that your attendance numbers are lower than you would prefer because most people don't show up all the time. In other words, too frequent of gatherings might mean you don't have the critical mass you're looking for at individual meetings. On the other hand, if you go too far the other direction and gather too infrequently, you also might see a drop-off in attendance because the group members are never quite sure if you're meeting and there isn't a sense of routine to your gatherings.

As the small-group leader, you want to find that Goldilocks zone for your group meeting frequency: not too frequent, not too infrequent; just right. If you find the right frequency, you can have some level of confidence that you'll have the critical mass you're looking for at most of your gatherings.

Again, each group is different. For some highly committed groups, a weekly gathering makes sense and will be well attended. For other groups, a weekly gathering is too frequent and might yield only 50 percent attendance. But twice a month could be a better fit and yield better-attended meetings. It's also true that depending on the season of year, you might need to be flexible on your frequency and critical mass expectations—for example, during the holidays or over the summer.

Critical mass and frequency of gatherings go hand in hand. Keep your focus on dialing in those two factors, and you'll keep your expectations healthy and set your group up for success.

But to repeat something I wrote in the introduction: *Just keep meeting.* You're not always going to hit your critical mass or frequency preferences. Those factors are variable. You as the leader are the constant. Just keep meeting and be happy to see whoever shows up.

Communication

As with attendance, communication needs to be properly calibrated. Too much communication or too little can be a problem. If you're contacting your group three or four times a week, they may start ignoring you. You become white noise against the backdrop of all the other messages and notifications in their lives. On the other hand, if you rarely contact the group outside of your meetings, you miss opportunities to encourage attendance and communicate important logistical information they might need to know.

Your goal should be to communicate frequently enough that your group feels informed and encouraged. Too infrequent and they feel ignored. Too frequent and they feel bombarded.

In my experience, once a week is a good frequency. This is true whether your group meets weekly or a couple times a month. Keep the communications brief and meaningful. I suggest three things for communiqués between meetings:

1. A quick word of spiritual encouragement (maybe a follow-up on something you discussed in your last meeting)
2. Logistical information they might need for the next gathering (for example, a change of time or location)
3. An invitation for prayer requests

Be concise; this could be handled in a couple paragraphs. For emails, my rule of thumb is this: When the reader opens your email, if they have to scroll down to see the bottom of the email where you sign your name, it's too long. If they can't see the bottom of your email when they open it up, they have no idea how long it is. If, however, they can see the whole email (including your signature) without scrolling down, they'll read it because they know it's concise.

But emails might not be the best method for your group. If text messages are better, use that. If a social media group is better, go with that. Use whichever method of communication will be most effective with your particular group. You might even ask your group at the outset which type of communication they would prefer, and let them know how frequently they can expect to hear from you between meetings. Help set their expectations even as you manage your own.

Co-Leaders

Another aspect of fostering your group's consistency (and spiritual growth) is raising up other leaders. What you're trying to avoid is the scenario in which your group only meets if you're there and you're leading. If you find that to be the case, your group has become too dependent on you for its survival.

To offset that possibility, be on the lookout for one or two other people in your group who could step in occasionally to lead discussions—even if you're present. You want to give them opportunities to grow in their own leadership abilities, and allowing them the chance to lead a group meeting while you're present will legitimize them in the eyes of your other group members. Also, if you're there as a participant, it allows you to gain insights into what it feels like to be a part of your group when you're not the leader, and you're able to follow up with the other leader to give feedback on how his or her leadership came across.

If you take steps to do this, you will have someone who is experienced and willing to lead when you're sick or have to miss a gathering for some other reason. The group will not be entirely dependent on your presence to continue meeting. It's also possible your co-leaders will go on to lead other groups, which would be a great thing for the kingdom. God might use your leadership and encouragement to raise up a new leader who will go on to make a lasting impact on others for many years.

If a congregation is dependent on a particular pastor being the speaker each week in order for people to show up on Sundays, that church is probably immature, unhealthy, or both. Similarly, a small group may be unhealthy or immature if it is entirely reliant on a particular person being there and leading every time. Still, it is best for you as the leader to be present and lead most of the time.

Time and Location

Once again, we need to reiterate that every group has its own culture. The right time and location of the meeting will be dependent on the size of the group and the life stage of most of the members. If the group is made up of young families, the location probably needs to be a house that's large enough to have a dedicated play area for the kids. The group also couldn't meet too late into the evening because of kids' bedtimes.

If the group is made up of college students, adults without kids, or empty nesters, there are a lot more options. The group could meet early in the morning or later in the evening. It could also be somewhere more public, like a restaurant or coffee shop, since there are no requirements for kids' space. I know of a men's group in my community that meets at a local breakfast spot. Because they meet there every Saturday morning, the restaurant manager has agreed to give them free unlimited coffee along with the breakfast that they purchase.

It's wise to choose a meeting space that is convenient for your group in terms of location, and also one that has the right environment—that is, it's conducive for conversations. You don't want to choose a location that is too loud or prone to overcrowding. It's also a good idea to have one or two backup locations in case your primary venue isn't available. Sometimes it works to rotate between the homes of group members so that no one person hosts too often. The downside of that option, however, is that it leaves the group with the ever-present question, "Where are we meeting again?"

Childcare

Childcare is one of those challenges that most small-group ministries struggle to address. The best approach is a proactive one, even if it's not a perfect one. If your group has families with small children who need childcare during the group meeting, this of course will need to be taken into consideration when planning the time and location of your gathering. Start the conversation about childcare with the parents in your group as early as possible to make sure everyone is on the same page and on board with whatever solution makes sense for your group.

If your group is part of a church-wide small-group ministry, your church may already have a solution in place (e.g., a childcare reimbursement program or an activity at a church facility where the kids can be dropped off during the group meeting). One option I've seen work well is having group members chip in to pay a babysitter to watch the kids at the house during each meeting. The best practice on that approach is to have the parents pay up front for a season of group meetings so that you don't have to remind them to chip in at every gathering. For example, if the babysitter would charge $25 per gathering, and your group will be meeting twelve times during the fall, that's $300 total. If there are five families in your group who will be availing themselves of the babysitting, have them each bring $60 to the first meeting.

In some cases, a babysitter isn't needed because older kids can watch the younger ones. If this isn't an option and the group doesn't want to pay a babysitter each week, the group members themselves can take turns watching the kids. That's not an ideal choice, but for some groups it's the best option.

The main point is this: Be proactive about finding a solution for the childcare needs of your group. If you wait too long or just try to figure it out each week, it won't work and will become burdensome for you, the parents, and—if you meet at someone else's home—the host.

There are of course other logistical hurdles that face many small-group leaders, but the areas we've covered in this chapter seem to be the most common. If you invest the time to think and pray about these areas at the beginning of your group's life, your effort will pay dividends in the long run.

4

Personal Challenges

Let's assume for a moment that you've embraced what we've covered so far: You have a biblical and realistic view of your role as the small-group leader. You've figured out the right frequency for your group meetings. You've dialed in your approach to communication. Logistical matters have been attended to. All that's left is to actually meet with your group members. Easy, right?

Not exactly. Many of the challenges that face small-group leaders are not logistical in nature, but personal: conflicts, flakiness, people monopolizing conversations, etc. If you lead small groups for any length of time, you will find that your groups are populated with not only people you love and get along with, but also people who irk you. You will spend time with all varieties of gossipers, contrarians, and chronic complainers, and sometimes that complainer will be you. We are human beings who effortlessly think of ourselves first, and in a small group you get a front row seat to this reality.

In this chapter, we're going to think about four personal challenges that are common to small groups. Not every small group will experience every one of these challenges, but long-term small-group leaders will inevitably encounter all of them in a variety of disguises.

I do, however, want to make a few general comments about handling interpersonal challenges within your group before I get into the specific examples.

First, if you get the impression that you've offended someone or you sense a relational distance between you and someone in your group, go directly to that person and speak privately about it—maybe before or after one of your group meetings. Maybe someone who used to be very engaged and positive has stopped speaking up at the group meetings or says only negative things. Perhaps someone is missing meetings more than usual—without explanation—or his or her inter-actions with you have become sparse or uncharacteristically matter-of-fact. These kinds of subtle changes may be indica-tors that there is something going on beneath the surface. As the leader, you should be the one to take the initiative and start an open conversation about it. It's as simple as saying something like this:

"Hey, I may be misreading things, but lately it feels like you might be upset at me about something. Or maybe it has nothing to do with me and you're just struggling. Either way, I'd like to know if you're willing to tell me. Is something going on?"

Initiating a conversation like that is very much in the spirit of what Jesus said: "If your brother or sister sins, go and point out their fault, just between the two of you. If they listen to you, you have won them over" (Matthew 18:15). You should seek out this conversation as early as possible after you begin to sense something might be wrong. Don't wait and hope that it goes away; in my experience, it doesn't. Your tone should be honest and clear, but also gentle and compassionate. Be prepared to listen more than you speak.

There may also be occasions in which you need to be the peacemaker between two members of your group. Again, address the issue early, directly, and gently. Peacemaking is not easy, but we can find comfort that we're doing the right thing, as Jesus said in the Sermon on the Mount: "Blessed are the peacemakers, for they will be called children of God" (Matthew 5:9). If you are a peacemaker, you will be called a child of God—in other words, you will be exhibiting one of God's family traits.

Now let's look at those four personal challenges that are common to small groups.

Needy People

If you lead small groups, you will encounter needy people. It's important, however, to distinguish between people who are *in need* and *needy people*. People who are in need are not a problem for your group or a distraction to be managed. These are brothers and sisters in Christ who are going through something difficult like a death in the family, loss of employment, illness, a relationship breaking apart, or economic hardship. They need the care and support of their church family, and your group has the privilege of walking with them through dark valleys. If you have people in need in your group, remember God's heart toward those who are suffering, expressed so often in the Psalms:

> The Lord is close to the brokenhearted and saves those who are crushed in spirit.
>
> Psalm 34:18

You, Lord, hear the desire of the afflicted; you encourage them, and you listen to their cry.

Psalm 10:17

Needy people, on the other hand, are indeed a problem for your group. Needy people are those who are perpetually expecting the group to help them with all sorts of things that are typical to life—general busyness, getting errands done, being tired, etc. They tend to present their own personal needs as the most important thing going in the group, and they have a knack for steering the group discussions back to themselves whenever possible. In my experience, needy people aren't really aware that they're doing this.

Needy people can hurt a group's long-term health because their presence hinders the discussions and makes it difficult for other group members to be honest about their own struggles. It is very important, therefore, to apply the principles covered earlier in this chapter: Be proactive, and have a private, honest conversation with them as soon as possible. And remember to be gentle; don't begin the conversation with an accusatory tone or approach it like a reprimand. Assume they don't know how much they've made the group about themselves, and diplomatically let them know how they're coming across. It might be wise to loop a pastor into this conversation, or ask the advice of a seasoned small-group leader, if you feel out of your depth.

As you confront the problem of needy people in your group, make sure to examine your heart before speaking with them about it. If your attitude toward them is something like *They're so annoying and they're messing up my group*, you might need to ask the Lord to soften your heart toward them and discover some compassion before beginning a conversation.

Remember Paul's words about this in his letter to the Ephesian Christians: "Be completely humble and gentle; be patient, bearing with one another in love. Make every effort to keep the unity of the Spirit through the bond of peace" (Ephesians 4:2–3).

Monopolizers

Another challenging type of group member is a *monopolizer*. Monopolizers tend to come in two varieties: (1) those who are quarrelsome, and (2) those who are not argumentative but by virtue of their personality tend to dominate the conversation.

Monopolizers of the first type are prone to argue. They almost seem to enjoy it, taking a contrarian position to almost anything the group seems to agree on. They come across as skeptical or cynical about most things, and they seem to want to be the center of attention.

Again, your job is to address the issue in a direct and gentle way, giving them grace as you do. Assume that they don't realize how they're coming across. They may feel like they're just contributing to the discussions in meaningful ways. Encourage them for the helpful things they do say, but let them know how their attitude or other negative comments are undermining their helpful comments.

Monopolizers of the second type are not necessarily argumentative and don't seem very cynical or skeptical. They may in fact be soft-spoken and kind. But they still have the capacity to dominate the conversation, because they ramble or seem to feel like they must weigh in on every single point or have the last word. Once again, they may not be aware of how they're coming across. They probably think they're just actively participating in the conversation.

This second type of monopolizer may not need a direct, private conversation. During the group discussion itself, you can subtly encourage them to pull back by listening to their comments and then using a transitional phrase like, "Let's hear from someone else. . . ." You could also pull them aside after the meeting and ask for their assistance in encouraging other group members to speak up. This will help them know to speak less while simultaneously making them feel valued and included in your effort to foster a healthy group discussion.

Gentleness is the operative word when confronting monopolizers (and other troublesome group members). As the proverb says, "A gentle answer turns away wrath, but a harsh word stirs up anger" (Proverbs 15:1).

Awkward Silences

When you're leading your small group through a discussion, awkward silences are inevitable—especially when your group members are still getting to know each other. People are reluctant to be the first one to answer a question. This leads to an awkward silence. These quiet moments are not really a problem for your group unless you as the leader allow them to become a problem by rescuing the conversation. If you are uncomfortable with these silences and find yourself interjecting and answering your own question after five seconds of quiet, then you are teaching your group that if they just wait long enough, they won't have to speak up.

Instead, embrace the awkward silences! Ask a discussion question, and then just wait. Wait longer than you think you should. Twenty seconds can feel like an eternity while waiting for someone to speak up, but it's only twenty seconds. If you wait long enough, you'll find that people do speak up, and they learn the lesson that you'll just keep waiting until they do.

If the awkward silence is unusually long, just call the group's attention to it. Say something like, "I know someone is thinking something about this subject, and I'd like to hear it!" You might even go get a drink refill or something, and say, "When I get back, let's talk about this."

If you can, during your group discussions, try to make your own contributions a follow-up to someone else's comment. Get in the habit of prefacing your own comment by building up the person who spoke before you. You could say something like, "That was a really insightful comment, Jeff. I hadn't really thought about it that way. That actually ties into something I've been thinking about. . . ." This helps develop a rapport with your group that you actually want to hear what they have to say and that you view yourself as learning from them.

Another way to break an awkward silence is to ask the question another way. For example, if the question was "What do you think it means to trust God?" you could wait fifteen seconds and then rephrase it: "Let's try this. Give me an example of a time you trusted God, or maybe a time you didn't—what did you learn from the experience?"

James's words are helpful when it comes to awkward silences and group discussions in general: "My dear brothers and sisters, take note of this: Everyone should be quick to listen, slow to speak and slow to become angry" (James 1:19).

As the group leader, be quick to listen to your group members. Don't be in a rush to rescue the discussions from silence. Be slow to speak. Don't view the discussions as opportunities for you to speak; view them as opportunities to listen. And be slow to become angry. Don't let clumsy conversations or challenging group members get under your skin. It's not about you having a stress-free experience. Trust that the Lord is working, and just keep moving forward.

Slow-Growing (Or No-Growing) Friendships

This last challenge is mainly about managing your own expectations rather than the actions or attitudes of your group members. Most leaders want the people in their group to become great friends. And some long-term meaningful friendships will blossom out of your small groups. I have many friendships today that grew out of a small group.

But there will be people who only attend your group and don't really invest in relationships outside of your group meetings, and that's okay. Some of them are introverts and don't need any additional friendships. Some are busy and don't have time for investment outside of the group meeting time.

Some friendships will grow, but at a slower rate than you would expect or prefer. It's okay. Don't take it personally if some people in your group are not becoming friends with everyone else or are doing so cautiously. God wired each of us to think and relate in unique ways, and he will use your group members' differences to accomplish his purposes in your small group and sharpen you as the leader.

The pain comes when you expect everyone in your group to become great friends very quickly and they don't. When that happens, you can easily wonder if you're failing as a leader when you're not. God may in fact be doing something powerful in the hearts of your group members—something you can't see yet. Just trust him as he works. Be the constant and keep meeting.

As you think about and address all of these personal challenges in your group, ask the Lord to give you a gracious, Christlike posture toward yourself and your group. As Paul put it: "Bear with each other and forgive one another if any of you has a grievance against someone. Forgive as the Lord forgave you" (Colossians 3:13).

Jesus is both your example and your source of strength as you lead, and that's a comforting thought you can cling to.

5

Spiritual Concerns

So far, our conversation about leading small groups has been mainly pragmatic. We've now reached a turning point, however, and will begin speaking of spiritual matters. In the following chapters, we will explore twelve biblical subjects that will provide a basic theological foundation for leading your group spiritually. But before we get into that material, we need to spend one more (brief) chapter on the mechanics of leadership. As a prelude to our biblical discussions in part 2, we need to spend some time on how to think about spiritual leadership. Think of this chapter as a leadership lens to look through as you apply the biblical truths we discover in the rest of the book.

How should I prepare for the group discussion?

You should be prepared for your group discussion, but not *too* prepared. If you are doing a Bible study, for example, familiarize yourself with what the discussion will be about for your next meeting. I would suggest reading the biblical text at least once before the group meeting, but please resist the urge to study it in depth before the group meeting and come up with all the answers you think you'll need. If you get into that habit, you will exhaust yourself in the long run and rob yourself of the joy of experiencing the study in real time with your group members.

Another unintended consequence of over-preparation is the creation of a teacher/student dynamic in your group, which will stifle discussions because your group members will feel that you (as the teacher) already have all the answers. You want your group members to see you wrestling with the material alongside of them—asking honest questions and wondering about how to personally apply the biblical text. So be prepared, but not too prepared. Don't try to become an expert on the material; just be a couple steps ahead of the group. Whatever preparation you do should be focused mainly on praying for your group meeting, and perhaps coming up with a handful of insightful open-ended questions you can ask during your discussion.

What if someone asks a question I can't answer?

People *will* ask questions you did not expect and questions you don't know how to answer. Some of them will be specific biblical questions, others real or hypothetical questions about life. Sometimes you will know what to say. Other times you won't, and that's okay. Once again, your goal is not to present yourself as some omnicompetent persona, but rather to set an example. In this case, you want to model for your group members what it looks like to search for and find answers to difficult questions. Show them how you will investigate. Teach them how to find the answers they're looking for!

You could consult a study Bible or commentary together. You could send a message to a pastor during the group meeting and then forward the response to the group when it comes in. Similarly, you could reach out to a professor at a local seminary or even invite one to join you at your next group meeting.

If you don't want to lose too much momentum during the group meeting by getting stuck on one question, you could tell your group that you'll seek the answer and bring your findings to the next group meeting.

Remember, your role is not to be a real-time biblical scholar or theologian. Your role is to *lead* your group—to show them how to follow and trust Jesus in the choppy waters of life. Encourage them to ask the tough questions and show them how to find true answers. Our God is not rattled by our questions, and you shouldn't be flustered by your group's questions either.

What if I am going through something painful and it's hard to imagine leading well?

You—just like your group members—will go through seasons of life that are painful and overwhelming. Once again, set an example for your group. Not an example of having everything together or putting on a brave face, but an example of how to respond to suffering. Show your group what it looks like to turn *toward* Jesus—the Good Shepherd—in the dark valleys of life. Let them see you lead imperfectly. Let your guard down and ask for their prayers and help. Give your group members the opportunity to care for you. Have the humility to be served. If you do, they will trust you to do the same for them when they suffer.

PART TWO

STARTER
SMALL-GROUP
STUDIES

What to Expect in the Starter Studies

In the following chapters, we will cover twelve topics of spiritual importance—subjects you will think and speak about repeatedly if you lead small groups for any length of time. As I stated in the introduction, these studies are designed to do two things:

1. Prepare you to address important biblical questions that often arise in small-group discussions
2. Model how to approach your group meetings

Each chapter will be organized in three sections, corresponding to the three basic parts of any small-group meeting: Social, Study, and Prayer.

- The **Social** section will include a few memorable ice-breaker type questions designed to deepen personal relationships within your group. One of the questions will serve as a lead-in to the subject matter of the study.
- The **Study** section will include Scripture, brief sections of teaching material, and several open-ended discussion questions related to the biblical subject matter.
- The **Prayer** section will include a suggested prayer to pray at the end of the gathering, along with some ideas about how to handle prayer requests.

There is a temptation in small-group leadership to skip the spiritual preparation or view the pragmatic side of leadership as more important or pressing. That is not true. Small-group leadership is a spiritual endeavor with accompanying practical challenges. The purpose of a small group is spiritual growth alongside other believers. Your spiritual preparation as a leader is critical, so please do not neglect or rush through the second part of this book. I encourage you to walk through it on your own as a prelude to the launch of your group or to make it the basis of your group's first twelve meetings.

These twelve questions are fundamental to our faith, and when life presents its heaviest challenges, these are the kinds of questions that you and your group members will be asking. Practical leadership questions of critical mass, frequency of meetings, childcare, awkward silences, and the like will quickly be drowned out by the high emotional and spiritual volume of life's deepest soul-level questions. We must be prepared to lead spiritually, and we can be.

6

What Is God Like?

Social

A few questions to get your gathering started. This can be done during a meal or at the outset of your meeting.

- **Personal question:** Give us a quick snapshot of how things have been going since our last meeting—maybe a high and low point. (Everyone answers.)
- **Open-ended spiritual question:** What's something you feel God is teaching you right now? (A couple people share.)
- **Lead-in question to the subject of the study:** What are you like? Briefly describe yourself in the third person, as if someone else is describing you.

Study

What is God like? It's a fundamental question of faith. It's an important question for seasoned believers who are seeking to grow in their relationship with God, and it's significant for people who are wondering if God is even real. Our culture is full of unbiblical stereotypes about God: the docile old man with the white beard, the angry god waiting to zap us with his lightning bolt, the hippie drifter from Nazareth.

Think of any meaningful relationship in your life, maybe a close friend or family member. If someone asked you what that person is like, you would be able to answer. You would talk about his or her personality traits and values, why you enjoy spending time with that person, and perhaps some endearing (or not-so-endearing) quirks. You know what that individual is like. Similarly, if we are to have a meaningful relationship with God, we need to know what he is like.

We can't, of course, fully answer that question in this brief study because people spend lifetimes seeking to know the Lord more and more. But we can put ourselves on the *path* of knowing what God is like. When taking all of Scripture into view, we see some divine qualities continually reaffirmed about him: He is holy (which means set apart or sacred), he is eternal, he is the creator, he is all-powerful, and he is a community in himself (i.e., one God in three persons—Father, Son, and Holy Spirit).

These aspects of God's divine nature certainly impact our view of him, but in our experience they can sometimes seem more informational than relational. We don't necessarily feel like we know God better on a personal level by knowing these attributes.

For example, knowing about the office and powers of the United States presidency tells us something about the president. If you were living in America during the early 1860s, you might know a lot about Abraham Lincoln from press reports (e.g., his leadership style, his decision-making processes, etc.). And all of that information is important for knowing something about the presidency and about the man Abraham Lincoln. But it's not the whole story. It's not the same as *knowing* Abraham Lincoln as his children did. They knew how it felt to experience family life with Lincoln—to see his public attributes expressed on a personal level in their daily relationship with him and to know him as a loving father.

We don't want to know about God; we want to know God. We want to know him as he is and enjoy the kind of relationship with him that he wants us to have. There are a few starting points that will help put us on the path to knowing him in this way.

Love and Justice at the Same Time

In one of his letters, Jesus's disciple John gives us a profound statement of what God is like:

> Dear friends, let us love one another, for love comes from God. Everyone who loves has been born of God and knows God. Whoever does not love does not know God, because God is love.
>
> 1 John 4:7–8

- What stands out to you about this text?
- What is the difference between saying "God is loving" and "God is love" (as John wrote)? Why does the difference matter?

In Psalm 103, we see an expansion on similar themes.

> The Lord is compassionate and gracious, slow to anger, abounding in love. He will not always accuse, nor will he harbor his anger forever; he does not treat us as our sins deserve or repay us according to our iniquities. For as high as the heavens are

above the earth, so great is his love for those who fear him; as far as the east is from the west, so far has he removed our transgressions from us.

Psalm 103:8–12

- How does this psalm relate to what we just read in 1 John?
- What qualities of God are listed here? Which are the most meaningful to you?
- Anything surprise or challenge you about this text?

Throughout Scripture, God is presented as being full of love and compassion, while simultaneously being just and willing to punish sin. This is the picture painted by the psalmists as well as the prophets. For example, the prophet Nahum wrote:

The Lord is a jealous and avenging God; the Lord takes vengeance and is filled with wrath. The Lord takes vengeance on his foes and vents his wrath against his enemies. The Lord is slow to anger but great in power; the Lord will not leave the guilty unpunished. His way is in the whirlwind and the storm, and clouds are the dust of his feet.

Nahum 1:2–3

- What qualities of God are listed here? How do they contrast with what we read about God being love?
- Anything else stand out to you about this passage?

The apostle Paul also alludes in many places to the reality of God judging humanity. In his second letter to the Corinthian Christians, Paul wrote:

We must all appear before the judgment seat of Christ, so that each of us may receive what is due us for the things done while in the body, whether good or bad.

2 Corinthians 5:10

- How do you feel about the idea of Jesus as judge? Why do you think you feel that way?

God is love, and he is also just. How do we make sense of these seemingly contradictory qualities? How can we have any clear notion of what God is like? The answer is that we look to Jesus for our understanding of God.

Jesus Is Our Picture of God

When Jesus came to earth, he did so in order to pay the penalty for our sins, but also to make himself known and knowable. God did not want to remain a mystery to us. In the gospel of John, Jesus tells us that if you want to understand what God is like, look to him:

Philip said, "Lord, show us the Father and that will be enough for us."

Jesus answered: "Don't you know me, Philip, even after I have been among you such a long time? Anyone who has seen me has seen the Father. How can you say, 'Show us the Father'?"

John 14:8–9

Jesus made it clear: To see him is to see God. The author of Hebrews spoke about the same reality:

In the past God spoke to our ancestors through the prophets at many times and in various ways, but in these last days he has spoken to us by his Son, whom he appointed heir of all things, and through whom also he made the universe. The Son is the radiance of God's glory and the exact representation of his being, sustaining all things by his powerful word. After he had provided purification for sins, he sat down at the right hand of the Majesty in heaven.

Hebrews 1:1–3

In Colossians we read something similar:

The Son is the image of the invisible God, the firstborn over all creation.

Colossians 1:15

In John, Jesus said that anyone who has seen him has seen the Father. In Hebrews, Jesus is described as the exact representation of God's being. In Colossians, he is the image of the invisible God.

- Which of these phrases speaks to you the most? Confuses you? Inspires you?

If Jesus is our picture of God, then we have to ask one more question: What is Jesus like?

Full of Grace and Full of Truth

In the prologue to John's gospel, he writes about Jesus (whom he calls "The Word"):

The Word became flesh and made his dwelling among us. We have seen his glory, the glory of the one and only Son, who came from the Father, full of grace and truth.

John 1:14

Grace is undeserved favor—God's gift to us (we will talk more about that in the next session). Truth is God's view of things, which we discover in Scripture. Jesus was full of both grace and truth at the same time. Not 50 percent of each, but 100 percent full of both. The grace side of the equation led Jesus to defend a woman caught in adultery. The truth side of the equation led him to tell her to leave her life of sin. The grace side of Jesus is displayed in the father character in the parable of the prodigal son, welcoming home his wayward son whom he never stopped loving. The truth side of the ledger led that father to say that the son had been dead and lost in his sin.

- Can you think of any other examples from Scripture of God being simultaneously full of grace and full of truth?
- How does it make you feel to know that Jesus is full of both grace and truth?
- How can we think in terms of grace and truth when dealing with conflict?

What is God like? As we have discovered, he is love and he is just—at the same time, which is what we see in the life of Jesus, who was the exact representation of God, full of grace and truth.

- How does all of this change your view of God?
- What questions do you still have about what God is like?

How should we respond to this? How should we relate to God? What kind of relationship has God invited us into? The writer of Hebrews tells us, speaking of Jesus as our great high priest:

Therefore, since we have a great high priest who has ascended into heaven, Jesus the Son of God, let us hold firmly to the faith we profess. For we do not have a high priest who is unable to empathize with our weaknesses, but we have one who has been tempted in every way, just as we are—yet he did not sin. Let us then approach God's throne of grace with confidence, so that we may receive mercy and find grace to help us in our time of need.

Hebrews 4:14–16

Jesus, our high priest—the exact representation of God, the visible image of the invisible God—is able to sympathize with us. He understands what it's like to be us, and invites us into an unhindered relationship with him. We can approach the throne of grace with confidence!

Summary

Question: What is God like?

Answer: Look to Jesus and find out.

Leader tip: When members of your small group seem to be struggling to know God, or they speak of God as if he's a mystery, remind them to look to Jesus as their way to know God. Encourage them to read the gospel of John, for example, to reencounter what Jesus said and did.

Prayer

1. Starting with yourself, ask the group for two things:
   - A quick update on any ongoing prayer requests
   - New prayer requests
2. Write down the prayer requests as people share:

3. Ask someone in the group to close your meeting with prayer.
   - **Sample prayer:** Lord Jesus, we want to know you as you are. We don't want to know stereotypical or convenient versions of you. We want to understand your nature on an informational level, but more importantly, we desire to know you and know about you on a relational level. Help us to find encouragement in the fact that you are love. Help us to discover a sense of wonder and reverence at the knowledge that you are just. Help us, Lord Jesus, to understand what it means that you came to earth full of grace and truth, and show us how we can interact with others in grace and truth. We need you, Holy Spirit, to shape our hearts and lead us into a deeper relationship with you. We ask you to do that, in Jesus's name. Amen.
4. In the next day or so, send a message to your group with the specific prayer requests so that you can be praying for each other between now and the next meeting.

7

What Is Grace?

Social

A few questions to get your gathering started. This can be done during a meal or at the outset of your meeting.

- **Personal question:** Give us a quick snapshot of how things have been going since our last meeting—maybe a high and low point. (Everyone answers.)
- **Open-ended spiritual question:** What's something you feel God is teaching you right now? (A couple people share.)
- **Lead-in question to the subject of the study:** What is the greatest gift you've ever received, and why did it mean so much to you?

Study

In the previous session, we saw that Jesus came full of grace and full of truth. That word *grace* is one of the most important and commonly used words in our lives of faith. It shows up consistently in sermons and worship songs, and we encounter it throughout the New Testament. But what is grace, and why does it matter?

The English word *grace* is a translation of the Greek word χάρις (*charis*). It's a word that is generally used to mean "favor." The Greek word *charis* is even translated into English as "favor" at several important moments in the New Testament. For example, in the gospel of Luke we read:

> But the angel said to her, "Do not be afraid, Mary; you have found favor [*charis*] with God. You will conceive and give birth to a son, and you are to call him Jesus.
>
> Luke 1:30–31

Thus, one element of grace is to understand that it has to do with God showing us favor. Another important element is the gift aspect. Grace, in the New Testament understanding, is God's favor given to us as a gift, which of course implies it cannot be earned. In fact, there is a related word in the New Testament, χάρισμα (*charisma*), which is often translated as "gift." For example, when Jesus's disciple Peter wrote his letter that we call 1 Peter, he used both words in one verse:

> Each of you should use whatever gift [*charisma*] you have received to serve others, as faithful stewards of God's grace [*charis*] in its various forms.
>
> 1 Peter 4:10

We see that the Greek word for *grace*—*charis*—and related words convey the dual ideas of favor and gift. Thus, a good working definition of *grace* is "God's gift of undeserved favor."

- What does this concept of grace mean to you?

The apostle Paul spoke often of God's grace. In Romans, Paul describes the gift of God's love that we did not deserve:

> You see, at just the right time, when we were still powerless, Christ died for the ungodly. Very rarely will anyone die for a righteous person, though for a good person someone might possibly dare to die. But God demonstrates his own love for us in this: While we were still sinners, Christ died for us.
>
> Romans 5:6–8

- Where in these verses do you see the *favor* aspect of grace?
- Where do you see the *gift* aspect?
- Where do you see the *undeserved* element?

In perhaps the most famous text on grace, we see Paul speak explicitly about how we are saved and the role grace plays:

> For it is by grace you have been saved, through faith—and this is not from yourselves, it is the gift of God—not by works, so that no one can boast.
>
> Ephesians 2:8–9

- What stands out to you about these verses?
- How do these verses impact your view of yourself? Of God?

We receive God's grace for salvation by putting our faith in Jesus. By trusting Christ. That is the only prerequisite for receiving the undeserved gift of God's saving grace. But we don't always live as if this is true. There are two twin challenges that relate to God's grace—one has to do with how we experience it, and the other has to do with how we show it to others.

The Problem of Receiving Grace

We live in a world that is oriented around achievement and getting what we deserve. God's grace does not make sense in that environment. The result is that we try to earn God's gift of grace or make ourselves worthy of it, which is impossible because it is—by definition—undeserved favor given to us by God as a gift. Deserving grace is not part of the equation. We are meant to enjoy our standing with God, resting in the knowledge that we have received his grace through Christ. As Paul put it in Romans 5:

> Therefore, since we have been justified through faith, we have peace with God through our Lord Jesus Christ, through whom we have gained access by faith into this grace in which we now stand.
>
> Romans 5:1–2

- How does grace allow us to have peace with God?
- What do you think it means to stand in grace, as Paul put it?

We must ask the Holy Spirit to allow us to understand his grace and enjoy the freedom and peace it is meant to give us. But even if we embrace God's grace for ourselves and understand that it is a gift we don't deserve, we still run the risk of being stingy in extending it to others.

The Problem of Extending Grace

Sometimes we forget key aspects of God's grace. We forget our own ongoing need for it, and we forget that it is God's gift to give. When others are sinning or we feel that they are undeserving of God's love for one reason or another, we can easily find ourselves judging them, forgetting that grace is undeserved in the first place. Grace is only extended to people who are undeserving, which is all of us.

The prophet Jonah, though mainly known because of the incident with the fish, is really one of our best examples of the challenges related to extending grace. Jonah was sent to Nineveh, a pagan enemy of Israel, with God's message of judgment. When the people of Nineveh responded with repentance—imperfect and perhaps ill-motivated repentance—God relented and did not bring the destruction of the city that he had planned. Jonah responded as I suspect many of us would:

> But to Jonah this seemed very wrong, and he became angry. He prayed to the Lord, "Isn't this what I said, Lord, when I was still at home? That is what I tried to forestall by fleeing to Tarshish. I knew that you are a gracious and compassionate God, slow to anger and abounding in love, a God who relents from sending calamity. Now, Lord, take away my life, for it is better for me to die than to live."
>
> But the Lord replied, "Is it right for you to be angry?"
>
> Jonah 4:1–4

- What stood out to you about these verses?
- When you think about how we Christians respond to the culture around us, which of our words and actions might cause God to say to us, "Is it right for you to be angry?"

Jonah was angry that the Ninevites weren't going to get what they deserved. He was angry that God's grace was being extended to them. So God gave him an object lesson to help him understand:

Jonah had gone out and sat down at a place east of the city. There he made himself a shelter, sat in its shade and waited to see what would happen to the city. Then the Lord God provided a leafy plant and made it grow up over Jonah to give shade for his head to ease his discomfort, and Jonah was very happy about the plant. But at dawn the next day God provided a worm, which chewed the plant so that it withered. When the sun rose, God provided a scorching east wind, and the sun blazed on Jonah's head so that he grew faint. He wanted to die, and said, "It would be better for me to die than to live."

But God said to Jonah, "Is it right for you to be angry about the plant?"

"It is," he said. "And I'm so angry I wish I were dead."

Jonah 4:5–9

The book of Jonah concludes with a statement from God on grace:

But the Lord said, "You have been concerned about this plant, though you did not tend it or make it grow. It sprang up overnight and died overnight. And should I not have concern for the great city of Nineveh, in which there are more than a hundred and twenty thousand people who cannot tell their right hand from their left—and also many animals?"

Jonah 4:10–11

God was telling Jonah about his love for Nineveh, despite all the ways its people had sinned. The Lord made the Ninevites in his image, and they were confused—they couldn't tell their right hand from their left. God is a compassionate God, and he asked Jonah, "Should I not have concern for them?"

- What did you notice about how God handled this situation with Jonah?
- Who are your Ninevites—the people to whom it is hardest to show grace?

We struggle to receive God's grace (because we think we don't deserve it), and we struggle to extend it to others (because we think they don't deserve it). These attitudes reveal that we fundamentally misunderstand what grace is. Grace isn't about anyone deserving anything. It is about God's love for us expressed through the undeserved gift of his grace, offered through the death and resurrection of Jesus.

Summary

Question: What is grace?

Answer: God's gift of undeserved favor.

Leader tip: When members in your group seem to be striving to impress God or get on his good side, remind them what grace is all about! If they are struggling to show grace to someone else, help them remember their own need for God's grace, which can help propel them toward showing grace to others.

Prayer

1. Starting with yourself, ask the group for two things:
   - A quick update on any ongoing prayer requests
   - New prayer requests
2. Write down the prayer requests as people share:

3. Ask someone in the group to close your meeting with prayer.
   - **Sample prayer:** Lord Jesus, we ask for your help in understanding your grace. We want to experience the freedom and peace that come with your grace, but we confess that we still think of it in terms of deserving it. We struggle to feel we deserve it, and we struggle with extending grace to others. Jesus, we know that you came full of grace and truth, and we want to grow in looking more like you. We want to be molded and shaped in your image, and part of that is experiencing your grace and extending it to others in your name. Help us do that, Lord. Change us from the inside out. We trust you to do that work in our hearts. Amen.
4. In the next day or so, send a message to your group with the specific prayer requests so that you can be praying for each other between now and the next meeting.

8

How Does God View Me?

Social

A few questions to get your gathering started. This can be done during a meal or at the outset of your meeting.

- **Personal question:** Give us a quick snapshot of how things have been going since our last meeting—maybe a high and low point. (Everyone answers.)
- **Open-ended spiritual question:** What's something you feel God is teaching you right now? (A couple people share.)
- **Lead-in question to the subject of the study:** Have you experienced unconditional love in your life? How do you know if someone loves you unconditionally?

Study

We have already considered what God is like, which is critical because our views of God can become easily warped by the culture around us and our own interior musings about him. If our view of God is not tethered to Scripture and what he revealed about himself in the life of Christ, then we will inevitably view God in an unbiblical way, which leads to many varieties of confusion and discouragement.

Just as it is important to examine our view of God, we must also take time to reflect on how we believe God views us. It is possible to have a wonderful view of God—a biblical one—while simultaneously believing that the wonderful God of the Bible does not like us very much. Or that he is perpetually disappointed in us. Or that he is uninterested in our lives. Knowing how God views us provides durable reassurance as we experience the emotional roller coaster of life, and it helps us have an even deeper understanding of what God is like.

In this study session, we will cover four aspects of how God views us.

1. God Sees You As Someone Who Resembles Him

In the opening pages of the Bible, we read the creation account. God creates the heavens and the earth from nothing. He speaks galaxies and geckos into existence. And then he does something different:

> Then God said, "Let us make mankind in our image, in our likeness, so that they may rule over the fish in the sea and the birds in the sky, over the livestock and all the wild animals, and over all the creatures that move along the ground." So God created mankind in his own image, in the image of God he created them; male and female he created them.
>
> Genesis 1:26–27

- What do these verses tell you about how God might view you?

Theologians debate exactly what it means to have been created in God's image, but most agree it has something to do with dominion (i.e., ruling over creation), free will, and relationships. God is by nature a community (Father, Son, and Spirit), and our capacity as humans to have relationships with him and each other is reflective of God's nature. When God looks at everything in creation, he sees in us the only thing that bears a resemblance to him—the only creature made in his image.

- How does the knowledge that you bear God's image change your view of him? Of yourself?

Because we are so precious to God as his image bearers, he was willing to go to great lengths to rescue us from our sins. That leads us to our second point.

2. God Sees You As Someone Worth Dying For

On the eve of his arrest and crucifixion, Jesus spoke to his disciples. He encouraged them, prayed for them, and spoke about their future lives of faith. He also made sure they knew that they were loved. In the gospel of John, we read these words of Jesus:

> "As the Father has loved me, so have I loved you. Now remain in my love. If you keep my commands, you will remain in my love, just as I have kept my Father's commands and remain in his love. I have told you this so that my joy may be in you and that your joy may be complete. My command is this: Love each other as I have loved you. Greater love has no one than this: to lay down one's life for one's friends."

> John 15:9–13

- What do these verses tell you about how God views you?
- What did Jesus want his followers to grasp about his upcoming execution?

At the beginning of Paul's letter to the Galatians, he said this about Jesus's mission:

> To the churches in Galatia: Grace and peace to you from God our Father and the Lord Jesus Christ, who gave himself for our sins to rescue us from the present evil age, according to the will of our God and Father, to whom be glory for ever and ever. Amen.
>
> Galatians 1:2–5

- According to Paul, why did Jesus die?
- If you were lost or in danger and someone rescued you, how would you feel toward your rescuer? Do you think of God as your rescuer?
- How does it make you feel to know that God thought you were worth rescuing—at the cost of his Son's life?

These first two points are true of all human beings. God made every man and woman in his image. Secondly, God views every single person who has ever walked the earth as worth dying for.

But not everyone will respond to the gospel in faith by placing their trust in Christ for salvation. Many people have rejected or ignored—and will continue to reject or ignore—God and his offers of rescue and relationship. God still loves people who have rejected him, of course, but they are separated from him because of their sins.

The next two points are true of people who are *in Christ*, that is, those who have placed their faith in Jesus for salvation and have received forgiveness for their sins and the promise of eternal life.

3. If You Are in Christ, God Sees You As a New Creation

Paul writes in his second letter to the Corinthians:

If anyone is in Christ, the new creation has come: The old has gone, the new is here! All this is from God, who reconciled us to himself through Christ and gave us the ministry of reconciliation.

2 Corinthians 5:17–18

In the original Greek language of the New Testament, it reads a bit more literally: "If anyone is in Christ, (that one is) a new creation."

- What do you think it means to be viewed by God as a new creation? How is that different from being an improved creation?
- How does it make you feel to know that you're a new creation because of Christ?
- Why do you think it's important to remember that we are new creations in God's eyes?

While being a new creation is an important aspect of our spiritual identity and how God views us, there is one more missing ingredient: the relationship aspect. Does God view us as new creations in some impersonal way? Is he dying for us and remaking us from a distance? The fourth point of this session gives us the answer.

4. If You Are in Christ, God Sees You As His Child

In the prologue to the gospel of John, we read these remarkable words:

> To all who did receive [Christ], to those who believed in his name, he gave the right to become children of God—children born not of natural descent, nor of human decision or a husband's will, but born of God.

John 1:12–13

- What stands out to you about these verses?
- How does this text affect how you think God views you?

Paul speaks to the same idea in Romans:

> Those who are led by the Spirit of God are the children of God. The Spirit you received does not make you slaves, so that you live in fear again; rather, the Spirit you received brought about your adoption to sonship. And by him we cry, "Abba, Father." The Spirit himself testifies with our spirit that we are God's children.

Romans 8:14–16

- How do Paul's words relate to what we just read in John 1?

In one of the most moving moments in all of Jesus's teachings, we see this picture of being God's children in the parable of the prodigal son. After the son disrespects, dishonors, and abandons his father, he returns home to find not an angry father who shuns him, but a loving father who had been hoping all along that he would find his way home.

"While he was still a long way off, his father saw him and was filled with compassion for him; he ran to his son, threw his arms around him and kissed him."

Luke 15:20

- Do you imagine God having this kind of love for you? Why or why not?

In order to experience the joy and fullness of relationship with God, we must recalibrate not only our view of God, but our view of how God views us.

Summary

Question: How does God view me?

Answer: You resemble him. You're worth dying for. In Christ you're a new creation. In Christ you are God's child.

Leader tip: If any in your group are struggling with their self-worth or wondering if they are acceptable to God, remind them about how God views them. They are not defined by their actions or their past and present sins; each is a new creation, a beloved child of God.

Prayer

1. Starting with yourself, ask the group for two things:
   - A quick update on any ongoing prayer requests
   - New prayer requests

2. Write down the prayer requests as people share:

3. Ask someone in the group to close your meeting with
   prayer.
   • **Sample prayer:** Heavenly Father, we want to have a
     true view of you and a true view of how you view us.
     We confess that we often see you as distant or aloof
     or unimpressed with us. We struggle to think of you
     as a loving Father who delights in us. We fail to think
     of ourselves as beloved children and new creations,
     as you see us. We tend to still think of ourselves as
     flawed sinners who need to make ourselves worthy of
     your love, when you already demonstrated your love
     definitively and irrevocably on the cross. Shape our
     view of you, Lord, and shape our understanding of
     how you view us. Help that knowledge to give us joy
     in you. Amen.
4. In the next day or so, send a message to your group
   with the specific prayer requests so that you can be
   praying for each other between now and the next
   meeting.

9

What Does It Mean to Have Faith in God?

Social

A few questions to get your gathering started. This can be done during a meal or at the outset of your meeting.

- **Personal question:** Give us a quick snapshot of how things have been going since our last meeting—maybe a high and low point. (Everyone answers.)
- **Open-ended spiritual question:** What's something you feel God is teaching you right now? (A couple people share.)
- **Lead-in question to the subject of the study:** Tell us about someone you trust, and why you trust him or her.

Study

The English word *faith* can be problematic. Scripture teaches us that we are meant to have faith in God, but in the Western world—especially America—what we often think about when we hear the word *faith* does not exactly reflect the biblical concept.

American culture is achievement oriented and individualistic. When we hear statements like, "Have faith in God," what we tend to hear is, "Get good at having faith in God." We place the emphasis on ourselves to muster up a certain caliber or quality of faith so that God will take notice of us, answer our prayers, and generally treat us how we hope to be treated. Simply put, we work hard to be great at having faith.

But the biblical notion of faith is closer to our understanding of the word *trust*. If you trust in someone or something, the emphasis is not on your being good at having trust; the emphasis is on the trustworthiness of the person or thing in which you are placing your trust.

For example, if you were to ride a bicycle, you are demonstrating that you trust that bicycle to hold you up and function as it is supposed to. The bicycle's trustworthiness is not dependent on how much faith you have in the bicycle, as if your faith in the bicycle has some real effect on its sturdiness. No, the trustworthiness of the bicycle is based on its own qualities.

Likewise, our faith—our trust—in God should not mainly be about how good we are at having faith in him; it should be rooted in who God is and his own intrinsic trustworthiness.

Trusting in God places the emphasis on God and his trustworthiness, instead of the focus being on ourselves and how good we are at having faith in God.

- Why do you think it is important to nuance our understanding of what it means to have faith in God?
- What are the risks of having a self-focused faith in God as opposed to a God-focused trust in him?

- How might viewing your faith as an act of trust change how you relate to God?

When it comes to having faith in God—trusting in him—we tend to face recurring struggles in a few key areas: God's love, his presence with us, and his work in our lives. But we have every reason to trust God in these areas. At many times and in various ways, Scripture teaches us that:

1. God loves us.
2. God is present with us.
3. God is the one who transforms our lives.

Although we might affirm these truths, our actions and thoughts reveal that we don't trust that they're true. We find ourselves thinking and behaving as if we actually believe that:

1. God's love for us is not guaranteed.
2. God's presence with us is not certain.
3. God will transform our lives if we work hard enough.

- Which of these three ideas have you wrestled with the most?
- Why do you think it's been a struggle for you?

If having faith in God is about trusting him, we need to trust him in these key areas. We need to trust that God does love us. Even though God's love for us is clear in Scripture, we often feel as if we have to make ourselves worthy of his love or prove ourselves to him. But in 1 John—and other places in Scripture, such as Romans 5:8—we read that God's love for us was not dependent on us making ourselves lovable:

This is love: not that we loved God, but that he loved us and sent his Son as an atoning sacrifice for our sins.

1 John 4:10

- What stands out to you about this verse?
- What does this tell you about the nature of God's love?
- How does this verse help you trust in God?

We also need to trust that God is present with us. This is especially difficult to do when we are experiencing suffering in our lives, because we (mistakenly) assume that if we are struggling, then God must be far away or indifferent to our pain. We wonder if God is near and ask for more of his presence, even though Scripture teaches us that the Holy Spirit dwells within us:

You, however, are not in the realm of the flesh but are in the realm of the Spirit, if indeed the Spirit of God lives in you. And if anyone does not have the Spirit of Christ, they do not belong to Christ. But if Christ is in you, then even though your body is subject to death because of sin, the Spirit gives life because of righteousness. And if the Spirit of him who raised Jesus from the dead is living in you, he who raised Christ from the dead will also give life to your mortal bodies because of his Spirit who lives in you.

Romans 8:9–11

- What stands out to you about these verses?
- How does this text help you trust God?

We also need to trust God in the area of our personal spiritual growth. Even though Scripture teaches us that God is the one who transforms us from the inside out, we easily find ourselves striving to be the best we can be so that God will be impressed with our efforts and work in our lives. When we do this, we are relying on our own strength for transformation instead of trusting that God will do his transformative work in us. As Jesus said in John 15:

> "Remain in me, as I also remain in you. No branch can bear fruit by itself; it must remain in the vine. Neither can you bear fruit unless you remain in me. I am the vine; you are the branches. If you remain in me and I in you, you will bear much fruit; apart from me you can do nothing."
>
> John 15:4–5

- According to Jesus, how much can we do without him?
- How does this text help you trust God?

We cannot grow or change in our own strength. God is not there to help boost our efforts; he is the one who transforms lives.

Having faith in God is not about our skill at having faith; it's about trusting him. *Really* trusting him, which comes from a deep sense of who he is and why he is trustworthy. As the famous words of Proverbs put it:

> Trust in the Lord with all your heart and lean not on your own understanding; in all your ways submit to him, and he will make your paths straight.
>
> Proverbs 3:5–6

God will make our paths straight as we trust in him, not as we work to be good at having faith in him. We must ask God to cultivate a deep and resilient trust in our hearts—the sort of trust we see so often displayed in the Psalms. A trust that can weather the storms of life and the ups and downs of our emotions. If we do that, we will find joy and peace because we are resting in him. Our faith is based on who he is, not who we are. As Paul put it in Romans:

> May the God of hope fill you with all joy and peace as you trust in him, so that you may overflow with hope by the power of the Holy Spirit.
>
> Romans 15:13

Summary

Question: What does it mean to have faith in God?

Answer: To trust him because he is God and he is trustworthy.

Leader tip: When members of your group seem to be speaking of faith as something they have to strive for or get good at, remind them that faith in God is about trusting in him because he is trustworthy. It's not about getting good at having faith.

Prayer

1. Starting with yourself, ask the group for two things:
   - A quick update on any ongoing prayer requests
   - New prayer requests

2. Write down the prayer requests as people share:

3. Ask someone in the group to close your meeting with prayer.
   - **Sample prayer:** Lord Jesus, we confess that sometimes we do not trust that you love us. We do not believe deep down that you are with us. We place our focus on working hard to have faith in you instead of trusting in you and relying on you. Holy Spirit, please renew our minds in this area. Transform our hearts. Help us to have a deep, abiding sense of your love for us and presence with us. We ask that this would be true of us as individuals, and that it would be true of our families and communities. Holy Spirit, we submit to your transforming work in our lives. Amen.

4. In the next day or so, send a message to your group with the specific prayer requests so that you can be praying for each other between now and the next meeting.

10

How Do I Grow Spiritually?

Social

A few questions to get your gathering started. This can be done during a meal or at the outset of your meeting.

- **Personal question:** Give us a quick snapshot of how things have been going since our last meeting—maybe a high and low point. (Everyone answers.)
- **Open-ended spiritual question:** What's something you feel God is teaching you right now? (A couple people share.)
- **Lead-in question to the subject of the study:** What do you think it means to grow spiritually, and how is it done?

Study

When someone encounters Christ and places faith in him for salvation, that person is instantly transformed—born again, as Jesus put it in John 3:3. In the words of Paul, we are a new creation because of Jesus (2 Corinthians 5:17). When we place our faith in Christ and are saved by his grace, we are no longer defined by our sin and our distance from God. Our sins have been forgiven, and we are now a part of God's family with an eternal, unshakable inheritance awaiting us.

That, however, is not the entirety of our transformation. Our initial response of faith to the gospel accomplishes our salvation, but God intends to continue working in our lives to grow us to look more and more like him. This is called sanctification, which is the process by which God transforms us—day by day, moment by moment—to think, act, and live in a way that reflects the inner transformation we received as a result of our salvation. Another way to talk about sanctification is to talk about our spiritual growth.

Spiritual growth—like trusting God—can seem daunting if we place the emphasis in the wrong place. If we think that our spiritual growth is mainly up to us, we will exhaust ourselves. If we believe that our sanctification is merely about following the rules and living a moral lifestyle, we will be disappointed and disenchanted. The truth is that our salvation was accomplished by God's work, and so is our spiritual growth.

In fact, Jesus spoke about coming to know him as a process of unburdening. Placing our lives in his hands should feel like rest. As Jesus said,

> "Come to me, all you who are weary and burdened, and I will give you rest. Take my yoke upon you and learn from me, for I am gentle and humble in heart, and you will find rest for your souls. For my yoke is easy and my burden is light."
>
> Matthew 11:28–30

- What did you notice about these verses?
- What do you believe these verses tell you about spiritual growth?
- Are these verses comforting to you or confusing?

From the perspective of the New Testament, the Old Testament can seem like a lot of rules, like our relationship with God is mainly about striving to be moral. The God of the Old Testament can sometimes seem — if we are not reading carefully—as if he is distant, detached, and lacking in compassion. But nothing could be further from the truth. The Psalms are full of declarations of God's kindness, compassion, and care for his people.

After the Israelites turned their back on God for generations and he exiled them to Assyria and Babylon, he spoke of his desire to bring them home into the Promised Land and into a restored relationship with him. And God spoke about how the people would be able to grow spiritually and live as he called them to live. It wouldn't be in their own strength; God would do the work in their hearts:

"I will take you out of the nations; I will gather you from all the countries and bring you back into your own land. I will sprinkle clean water on you, and you will be clean; I will cleanse you from all your impurities and from all your idols. I will give you a new heart and put a new spirit in you; I will remove from you your heart of stone and give you a heart of flesh. And I will put my Spirit in you and move you to follow my decrees and be careful to keep my laws. Then you will live in the land I gave your ancestors; you will be my people, and I will be your God."

Ezekiel 36:24–28

- What did you find interesting about these verses? Comforting? Confusing?
- Make a list of the things God says he will do for his people in this passage. Which ones speak to you the most?
- What will be the cause of people following God's decrees? How are they able to do it?

The indwelling Holy Spirit is the one who moves and enables God's people to act according to his will and his commands. We see this idea woven throughout the New Testament as well. In Romans 8, Paul speaks about this:

> You, however, are not in the realm of the flesh but are in the realm of the Spirit, if indeed the Spirit of God lives in you. And if anyone does not have the Spirit of Christ, they do not belong to Christ. But if Christ is in you, then even though your body is subject to death because of sin, the Spirit gives life because of righteousness. And if the Spirit of him who raised Jesus from the dead is living in you, he who raised Christ from the dead will also give life to your mortal bodies because of his Spirit who lives in you.
>
> Romans 8:9–11

As we continue reading Romans, we see this idea reemphasized over and over. The Holy Spirit supernaturally enables us to grow spiritually. In passages like Ezekiel 36:24–28 and Romans 8:9–11 that we just read, the Holy Spirit is spoken about explicitly; he lives within us and works for our transformation.

There are other places in Scripture that speak to the same idea, but we have to be looking closely to notice it. In some cases, we have to take notice of the grammar in the passage. Specifically, we have to pay attention to passages that speak about our spiritual growth in the passive voice. Grammatically speaking, the active voice refers to things we do—actions we take. The passive voice, by contrast, refers to actions that are done to us. Often, you can tell the passive voice is being used because it will have the word *be* before a verb. For example, instead of the verb *transform* (active voice), it will say *be transformed* (passive voice).

The passive voice means that God is doing something to us, rather than us doing something for ourselves. See if you can find the passive-voice verbs in the following two passages, both directly relating to our sanctification:

> And we know that in all things God works for the good of those who love him, who have been called according to his purpose. For those God foreknew he also predestined to be conformed to the image of his Son, that he might be the firstborn among many brothers and sisters.
>
> Romans 8:28–29

> I urge you, brothers and sisters, in view of God's mercy, to offer your bodies as a living sacrifice, holy and pleasing to God—this is your true and proper worship. Do not conform to the pattern of this world, but be transformed by the renewing of your mind. Then you will be able to test and approve what God's will is—his good, pleasing and perfect will.
>
> Romans 12:1–2

- What do you think it means to be conformed to the image of Christ (passive voice)? How is that different from conforming yourself to the image of Christ (active voice)?

- What do you think it means to be transformed by the renewing of your mind? How is this different from transforming yourself by renewing your mind?

The very grammar in these verses—the passive voice—teaches us that God is the one doing the transforming. He is the one conforming us to the image of Christ. We are not transforming ourselves or becoming Christlike. It is the Holy Spirit working within us and through us.

- How does this reality change your view of God and your relationship with him?

It's important at this point to note, however, that God still calls us to act and think in certain ways. God's moral laws are unchanging and universal, and we are called to act according to his commandments. Jesus's sermons and Paul's letters are full of encouragement and commands to live a certain way. So how do we reconcile these commands to make changes in our lives with the truth that the Holy Spirit is the one doing the heavy lifting in our spiritual growth? What does it look like to make choices that align with God's commands while still trusting that he is transforming us?

Jesus gives us some clear guidance in John 14. He speaks about the importance of following his commandments, and then he immediately tells us how this is possible:

> "If you love me, keep my commands. And I will ask the Father, and he will give you another advocate to help you and be with you forever—the Spirit of truth. The world cannot accept him, because it neither sees him nor knows him. But you know him, for he lives with you and will be in you. I will not leave you as orphans; I will come to you."
>
> John 14:15–18

- What stands out to you about this passage? How does it relate to what we've covered so far in this session?

Trusting God to bring about our spiritual transformation and making choices that align with his commands are not mutually exclusive; they go hand in hand. If we love God—if we have been saved by him and are yielding our life to him—then we will desire to keep his commands. We will make choices that align with his commandments, and we can do so resting in the knowledge that the Holy Spirit will empower us for the task.

On the subject of how God brings about our spiritual growth, I leave you with the words of the apostle Paul, who eloquently summarized what we've been exploring in this session:

> May God himself, the God of peace, sanctify you through and through. May your whole spirit, soul and body be kept blameless at the coming of our Lord Jesus Christ. The one who calls you is faithful, and he will do it.
>
> 1 Thessalonians 5:23–24

Summary

Question: How do I grow spiritually?

Answer: Make choices that align with God's commands, trusting that the Holy Spirit is the one who is transforming you and enabling you to live a God-honoring life.

Leader tip: When you see people in your small group struggling to grow and make choices that honor God, remind them that God does the heavy lifting in their spiritual growth. Encourage them to focus their prayers on trusting God and leaning on him.

Prayer

1. Starting with yourself, ask the group for two things:
   - A quick update on any ongoing prayer requests
   - New prayer requests
2. Write down the prayer requests as people share:

3. Ask someone in the group to close your meeting with prayer.
   - **Sample prayer:** Lord Jesus, I want to grow to look more like you. I want my life to be marked by obedience to your commands, and I want to resemble you more and more. Holy Spirit, I know that this is impossible without your presence and work in my life. Help me to make choices that will honor you, while not taking on too much of a burden or believing that I can transform myself. Help me to have a healthy, biblical view of my own spiritual growth, and give me the humility to submit to the transformative work you are doing in my heart and in my life. Amen.
4. In the next day or so, send a message to your group with the specific prayer requests so that you can be praying for each other between now and the next meeting.

11

What Is Sin and How Does It Affect My Life?

Social

A few questions to get your gathering started. This can be done during a meal or at the outset of your meeting.

- **Personal question:** Give us a quick snapshot of how things have been going since our last meeting—maybe a high and low point. (Everyone answers.)
- **Open-ended spiritual question:** What's something you feel God is teaching you right now? (A couple people share.)
- **Lead-in question to the subject of the study:** Finish this sentence: "Sin is _____." (Have the group members take a minute or so to think about their answers, and then have everyone share.)

Study

Sin is a subject of critical importance in our lives of faith, but it's not one that most of us are eager to discuss. Focusing on sin can bring us to two places we would prefer not to go: an honest assessment of our own sins—which is hard to do; or recognizing the sinful actions of someone else—which can make us feel judgmental or angry.

On the pop culture level, sin seems to be defined simply as doing immoral things. People might differ on what actions qualify as immoral, but there seems to be agreement that sins are immoral actions. But sinful actions are not uniformly portrayed as being negative. In the entertainment world, sinful actions are sometimes presented as being virtues, or something close to it. People who sin are portrayed as rebellious, independent, carefree, or iconoclastic—qualities that many find worthy of emulation.

There also seems to be a general agreement that everyone sins and that's just the way it is. We can't change it. No one is perfect.

When we look to the Scriptures, however, we find a very different, deeper picture of sin. We discover good news and bad news. The bad news is that sin is much worse than the pop culture understanding. The good news is that through Christ, the dominion of sin will not last forever. It has already been overwhelmed. It is being extinguished. It will be fully and finally defeated.

An important first step in understanding sin is to realize that the Bible speaks about sin in two main ways: as a *condition* we all share, and as *actions* we choose. We all start out sinners because we live in a fallen world, polluted by sin. The New Testament describes this condition as our *flesh*, sometimes translated as our *sinful nature*. It is a heart posture that is in continuous rebellion against God. As a result, we make specific sinful choices in our lives—thoughts, attitudes, actions, and inactions that are contrary to God's nature and will for our lives.

- What do you think about this twofold understanding of sin? Do you find it challenging? Enlightening? Discouraging?

In Paul's letter to the Galatians, he describes how our sinful nature (flesh) affects our actions, and he shows us how we are able to choose a different path because of Christ—the path of following the indwelling Holy Spirit.

> You, my brothers and sisters, were called to be free. But do not use your freedom to indulge the flesh; rather, serve one another humbly in love. . . .
>
> So I say, walk by the Spirit, and you will not gratify the desires of the flesh. For the flesh desires what is contrary to the Spirit, and the Spirit what is contrary to the flesh. They are in conflict with each other, so that you are not to do whatever you want. . . .
>
> The acts of the flesh are obvious: sexual immorality, impurity and debauchery; idolatry and witchcraft; hatred, discord, jealousy, fits of rage, selfish ambition, dissensions, factions and envy; drunkenness, orgies, and the like. I warn you, as I did before, that those who live like this will not inherit the kingdom of God.
>
> But the fruit of the Spirit is love, joy, peace, forbearance, kindness, goodness, faithfulness, gentleness and self-control. Against such things there is no law. Those who belong to Christ Jesus have crucified the flesh with its passions and desires. Since we live by the Spirit, let us keep in step with the Spirit.
>
> Galatians 5:13, 16–17, 19–25

- What did you notice about this passage? Anything surprise you?
- Paul speaks of our sinful nature as having been crucified when we give our lives to Christ (v. 24), but he also suggests that we can still choose to follow it instead of

the Spirit (v. 25). What do you think he means by this? How have you seen this play out in your spiritual life?

In Romans, Paul makes a detailed argument about the nature of sin and its role in our lives. He explains that we all have a sinful nature because of the original sin of Adam. He then contrasts Jesus with Adam and explains how Christ's sacrifice on the cross changed the game.

> Just as one trespass resulted in condemnation for all people, so also one righteous act resulted in justification and life for all people. For just as through the disobedience of the one man the many were made sinners, so also through the obedience of the one man the many will be made righteous. The law was brought in so that the trespass might increase. But where sin increased, grace increased all the more, so that, just as sin reigned in death, so also grace might reign through righteousness to bring eternal life through Jesus Christ our Lord.
>
> Romans 5:18–21

- How would you describe the relationship of sin and grace described in this passage?

After Paul makes this argument about the grace of God triumphing over sin, he takes on the next obvious question: If grace always wins over sin and we have grace through Jesus, why not just keep on sinning?

> What shall we say, then? Shall we go on sinning so that grace may increase? By no means! We are those who have died to sin; how can we live in it any longer? Or don't you know that all of us who were baptized into Christ Jesus were baptized into his death? We were therefore buried with him through baptism

into death in order that, just as Christ was raised from the dead through the glory of the Father, we too may live a new life.

For if we have been united with him in a death like his, we will certainly also be united with him in a resurrection like his. For we know that our old self was crucified with him so that the body ruled by sin might be done away with, that we should no longer be slaves to sin—because anyone who has died has been set free from sin.

Romans 6:1–7

- What do these first seven verses of Romans 6 seem to be saying about the place of sin in the life of a Christian?

In verse 6, Paul says that through Jesus we are no longer slaves to sin. This phrase is a clue to understanding how Paul is going to explain sin in the following verses. Sin is *personified* in this text as a slave master—a role that was well-known in the ancient Roman world where slavery flourished. Keep that in mind, and continue reading from Romans 6:11:

In the same way, count yourselves dead to sin but alive to God in Christ Jesus. Therefore do not let sin reign in your mortal body so that you obey its evil desires. Do not offer any part of yourself to sin as an instrument of wickedness, but rather offer yourselves to God as those who have been brought from death to life; and offer every part of yourself to him as an instrument of righteousness. For sin shall no longer be your master, because you are not under the law, but under grace.

What then? Shall we sin because we are not under the law but under grace? By no means! Don't you know that when you offer yourselves to someone as obedient slaves, you are slaves of the one you obey—whether you are slaves to sin, which leads to death, or to obedience, which leads to righteousness? But thanks be to God that, though you used to be slaves to sin, you have come to obey from your heart the pattern of teaching that has now claimed your allegiance. You have been set free from sin and have become slaves to righteousness.

Romans 6:11–18

The picture Paul is painting is that we are no longer *enslaved* to sin because of Christ. We still have a sinful nature, and we can still choose to sin, but we are not ruled by sin. It does not have dominion over us anymore. As my pastor growing up used to say, "We are not sinners. We are saints who sometimes sin."

- How does this concept change your view of sin?
- How does it encourage or challenge you?

Because of Jesus, our sinful nature no longer rules us, but we can still choose to sin—which is acting against our new nature in Christ. But what should we think when we observe others sinning or we ourselves make sinful choices?

First, we shouldn't judge others. As Paul said:

You, therefore, have no excuse, you who pass judgment on someone else, for at whatever point you judge another, you are condemning yourself, because you who pass judgment do the same things. Now we know that God's judgment against those who do such things is based on truth. So when you, a mere human being, pass judgment on them and yet do the same things, do you think you will escape God's judgment?

Romans 2:1–3

Second, we shouldn't be too hard on ourselves when we sin. If we are in Christ, then our sins have been dealt with completely on the cross. Of course it should grieve us when we sin—and we should repent—but we should never think that our relationship with God is in jeopardy or that we are defined by our sinful choices. We are no longer slaves to sin—though we sometimes sin. Sin does not rule us anymore. As Paul wrote in Romans 8:

> Therefore, there is now no condemnation for those who are in Christ Jesus, because through Christ Jesus the law of the Spirit who gives life has set you free from the law of sin and death.
>
> Romans 8:1–2

- If we have placed our trust in Christ for salvation, we are not subject to condemnation because of our sins. How does this change your life? Why is this sometimes hard to believe?

Summary

Question: What is sin and how does it affect my life?

Answer: Sin is a rebellion against God. It is a condition and also choices that we make. If we are in Christ, then we have been set free from sin's dominion, though we do still sin sometimes.

Leader tip: When people in your group struggle with sin and guilt in their lives, remind them that they are not enslaved to or defined by that sin, and because of Christ there is no condemnation waiting for them. Encourage them to ask God's help in overcoming their sinful choices, so that they can walk in step with the Spirit and their true identity as a child of God.

Prayer

1. Starting with yourself, ask the group for two things:
   - A quick update on any ongoing prayer requests
   - New prayer requests
2. Write down the prayer requests as people share:

3. Ask someone in the group to close your meeting with prayer.
   - **Sample prayer:** Lord Jesus, we confess that we underestimate the power of sin and we underestimate your power to overcome it. We thank you, Lord, that because of your grace, the power of sin to rule us has been broken. We ask your forgiveness for the many times we choose to sin in spite of our deliverance from it. Holy Spirit, we need you to enable us to walk in step with you. Left to our own devices, we will act as if sin still rules us even though it does not. Help us to trust in your love for us and the fact that there is no condemnation for those of us in Christ Jesus. Help us to cling to that hope, and to live accordingly. Amen.
4. In the next day or so, send a message to your group with the specific prayer requests so that you can be praying for each other between now and the next meeting.

12

How Should I Pray?

Social

A few questions to get your gathering started. This can be done during a meal or at the outset of your meeting.

- **Personal question:** Give us a quick snapshot of how things have been going since our last meeting—maybe a high and low point. (Everyone answers.)
- **Open-ended spiritual question:** What's something you feel God is teaching you right now? (A couple people share.)
- **Lead-in question to the subject of the study:** How would you describe your prayer life, and how does it compare with what you think the Bible says about prayer?

Study

Throughout Scripture, we are told that God desires, invites, and hears our prayers. For example, the psalmist writes:

As for me, I call to God, and the Lord saves me. Evening, morning and noon I cry out in distress, and he hears my voice.

Psalm 55:16–17

Despite knowing that God invites our prayers, we often struggle to know how to pray, what to pray, and what to expect from our prayer lives. In the West—especially in results-oriented cultures like America—we tend to have a utilitarian outlook on prayer: We pray to God to ask for his help with our problems. Of course, asking for God's help and provision is one important part of prayer, but a mostly pragmatic, problem-solving approach to prayer misses the deeper, more beautiful truth about prayer.

We are meant to have a relational outlook on prayer, not a practical one. As we pray, we can and should view God as a loving Father who cares deeply for us and wants to be invited into our hearts and minds. He wants to hear about our deepest pains and our grandest hopes. He wants to know the ways in which we feel we need his help. Just as loving parents want to hear about their child's struggles—though the parents may be unable or reluctant to intervene—God also wants to be there for us in our tough times. He also wants us to listen for his voice. Prayer is not mainly about solving problems; it's about experiencing and enjoying our relationship with God.

- What do you think about this?
- Has your prayer life been mainly pragmatic or relational? Why do you think that's the case?

Though prayer is relational—and thus, not formulaic—we do need to know something about how prayer works. In Matthew 6, we find the famous Lord's Prayer and some introductory comments Jesus made about it. In this text, we will discover a basic guide for how to pray, as well as some encouragement (and warnings) about our attitudes toward prayer.

How We Should Think about Prayer

"Be careful not to practice your righteousness in front of others to be seen by them. If you do, you will have no reward from your Father in heaven. . . . And when you pray, do not be like the hypocrites, for they love to pray standing in the synagogues and on the street corners to be seen by others. Truly I tell you, they have received their reward in full. But when you pray, go into your room, close the door and pray to your Father, who is unseen. Then your Father, who sees what is done in secret, will reward you. And when you pray, do not keep on babbling like pagans, for they think they will be heard because of their many words. Do not be like them, for your Father knows what you need before you ask him."

Matthew 6:1, 5–8

- What do you notice about these verses?
- Who is the audience of our prayers?
- What is the danger of making our prayers a performance?

A Guide for Prayer (Matthew 6:9–13)

"This, then, is how you should pray." These are the introductory words to the Lord's Prayer, and before we get into the prayer itself, it is important to notice a key word in this opening phrase: *how*. Jesus says that what he is about to tell us is an example for us. It is a guide to the manner in which we ought to pray. It is not a script. He did not say, "This then, is *what* you should pray." We should think of the Lord's Prayer as a rough outline or template that we can go through when we pray. It helps make sure our priorities are in order and that our heart is in the right place. Let's continue now with the prayer itself. Note especially the order of thoughts.

> "'Our Father in heaven, hallowed be your name, your kingdom come, your will be done, on earth as it is in heaven. Give us today our daily bread. And forgive us our debts, as we also have forgiven our debtors. And lead us not into temptation, but deliver us from the evil one.'"
>
> Matthew 6:9–13

- What is the basic idea of "Our Father in heaven, hallowed be your name"?
- What is the basic idea of "Your kingdom come, your will be done, on earth as it is in heaven"?
- What is the basic idea of "Give us today our daily bread"?
- What is the basic idea of "And forgive us our debts, as we also have forgiven our debtors"?
- What is the basic idea of "And lead us not into temptation, but deliver us from the evil one"?
- What does the order of these ideas tell you about how Jesus wants us to pray?

A number of biblical commentators and theologians over the centuries have recommended praying the Lord's Prayer line by line, and then elaborating on that idea with specifics from your own life. For example, you could pray something like, "Give us today our daily bread. Lord Jesus, you know what I need. Please help me to trust in your provision and to be thankful for all the things you've already given to me. Thank you for the job interview I have lined up for next week. . . ."

So the Lord's Prayer gives us a guide as to how we should pray. But it is mainly about the act of praying individual prayers. What about our prayer life in the long haul, over time? We can find some clues in something else Jesus said—in the parable of the persistent widow (Luke 18:1–6):

> Then Jesus told his disciples a parable to show them that they should always pray and not give up.
>
> Luke 18:1

The final phrase of verse 1 ("always pray and not give up") does not mean "always pray and just keep on praying," which would be one basic idea stated in two ways. The phrase conveys two separate, related ideas. The "not give up" part is a translation of a Greek word that has to do with being discouraged or losing heart. So we might translate that last phrase as "always pray and do not lose heart (or become discouraged)." Jesus is telling us that persistence in prayer and avoiding discouragement are linked. Then Jesus tells the parable of the persistent widow:

> He said: "In a certain town there was a judge who neither feared God nor cared what people thought. And there was a widow in that town who kept coming to him with the plea, 'Grant me justice against my adversary.'
>
> "For some time he refused. But finally he said to himself, 'Even though I don't fear God or care what people think, yet because this widow keeps bothering me, I will see that she gets justice, so that she won't eventually come and attack me!'"
>
> Luke 18:2–5

This widow, who has no power, pesters a self-centered, immoral judge for justice against an accuser. She is seeking vindication from the one who can provide it. And even though the judge is not a man of character, he gives her justice merely out of self-interest. It's a striking scene. Next, Jesus gives us the meaning of this parable:

> And the Lord said, "Listen to what the unjust judge says. And will not God bring about justice for his chosen ones, who cry out to him day and night? Will he keep putting them off? I tell you, he will see that they get justice, and quickly. However, when the Son of Man comes, will he find faith on the earth?"
>
> Luke 18:6–8

Jesus was saying that if even this unjust judge hears the pleas of the widow and responds, how much more will God—who is a just judge and loves his people—respond to the cries of his Church?

Jesus finishes with a rhetorical question: When the Son of Man (Jesus) returns, will he find faith on the earth? This question relates directly to prayer, which is what the parable of the persistent widow was about. Will Jesus find people who are still believing in him, praying, and trusting in him despite life's challenges?

The point is this: Our endurance in prayer—or lack thereof—tells us something about whether we really trust in God. When we continue praying over and over, it is a testament to the fact that we keep believing that God is real, that he's there, that he's listening, that he cares. It's not about praying the perfect words in a precise way with the perfect frequency. Even if our prayers are clumsy and intermittent, the mere fact that we keep praying is an expression of trust in God.

- What do you think about Jesus's parable of the persistent widow? How does it change your view of prayer?

- What do you think is the relationship between prayer and trusting God?

Our tendency—if we have a pragmatic view of prayer—is to start talking to God only when things get tough. Because we view God as our problem solver, we don't feel a need to talk to him outside of our requests. Praying like this would be like a teenager who rarely speaks to his parents unless he wants money or help with something he can't do on his own. There is no real relationship there. Or we do the opposite—we pray with regularity but *stop* talking to God when we encounter pain because we feel like God owes us a life with minimal suffering. In this case, we cease our prayers out of resentment toward God.

These kinds of prayer lives show that our trust in God is not rooted in who he is, but rather in what he can do for us.

A persistence and predictability to our prayers shows that there is a real, sturdy trust at the foundation of our relationship with God, which will help us avoid discouragement.

- Why is it hard to talk to God when we're struggling?
- Why is it difficult—on the other hand—to talk to God consistently when we're *not* struggling?

Our prayers are not performance pieces to be perfected. They are not meant to entertain or appease some impersonal God. Our prayers are real, honest conversations with a loving heavenly Father who wants to hear from us. We should always pray and not lose heart. As the psalmist put it,

I love the Lord, for he heard my voice; he heard my cry for mercy. Because he turned his ear to me, I will call on him as long as I live.

Psalm 116:1–2

Summary

Question: How should I pray?

Answer: Honestly and consistently, with the main goal being a deeper relationship with God.

Leader tip: When you hear group members speaking about prayer primarily as a way to ask God for things, remind them of the deeper reason to pray—to experience the joy of total, unhindered access to God and a relationship with him.

Prayer

1. Starting with yourself, ask the group for two things:
   - A quick update on any ongoing prayer requests
   - New prayer requests
2. Write down the prayer requests as people share:

3. Ask someone in the group to close your meeting with prayer.
   - **Sample prayer:** Lord Jesus, help me to pray more consistently, with greater honesty, and with the right heart—so that I can know you more deeply. Amen.
4. In the next day or so, send a message to your group with the specific prayer requests so that you can be praying for each other between now and the next meeting.

13

Where Is God When I Suffer?

Social

A few questions to get your gathering started. This can be done during a meal or at the outset of your meeting.

- **Personal question:** Give us a quick snapshot of how things have been going since our last meeting—maybe a high and low point. (Everyone answers.)
- **Open-ended spiritual question:** What's something you feel God is teaching you right now? (A couple people share.)
- **Lead-in question to the subject of the study:** When you're going through something really tough, what do you think of God? Do you picture him as distant, or especially close?

Study

When we experience pain in our lives, it reveals something about our trust in God. Do we turn *toward* him because we believe he loves us and cares about what we're going through, or do we turn *away* from him because we're not sure he's interested in us or we're angry at him for allowing us to experience suffering? It is normal and natural to ask God some honest and hard questions during times of pain, and as we'll see in this session, confronting God when we're suffering is actually quite biblical. The most important thing is that we turn toward him, even if it is with hard questions.

The Psalms consistently show us that God cares deeply for us, especially when we're going through a time of pain. For example:

The Lord is close to the brokenhearted and saves those who are crushed in spirit.

Psalm 34:18

- What do you think of these words? Are they comforting or hard to believe? Why?

When we're walking through sickness, relational turmoil, financial upheaval, pain, or loss, our emotional volume is turned way up. It is hard to think rightly about God during those times. We wonder why we're going through a tough season, and we have some honest questions for God that we're not sure we should ask. As a result, many of us just shut down, grit our teeth, and try to muddle through.

But we must remember that God is present with us, he loves us, and he invites total honesty from us. He knows our hearts anyway, so there's no use in pretending we feel something we don't. In fact, in Acts 15:8, God is described by a single Greek word, *kardiognōstēs* (καρδιογνώστης), that translates into English as "knower of hearts." There is no use pretending with God, and he doesn't ask us to.

A great example of this can be found in the Old Testament book of Habakkuk. The prophet Habakkuk lived during a tumultuous time in Israel's history, when the people had turned their backs on God and were facing invasion by powerful foreign adversaries. The prophet Habakkuk wonders why an all-powerful, loving God would allow suffering and injustice to occur, and he asks God about it. The book of Habakkuk takes the form of a dialogue between the prophet and God, and the prophet begins with some very direct, unfiltered questions:

How long, Lord, must I call for help, but you do not listen? Or cry out to you, "Violence!" but you do not save? Why do you make me look at injustice? Why do you tolerate wrongdoing? Destruction and violence are before me; there is strife, and conflict abounds. Therefore the law is paralyzed, and justice never prevails. The wicked hem in the righteous, so that justice is perverted.

Habakkuk 1:2–4

- What do you think of Habakkuk's questions?
- Have you ever asked God anything like this? Why or why not?
- Why do you think people feel uneasy speaking to God with such honesty?

If we keep reading chapter 1 of Habakkuk, we see God's reply. He is going to help Habakkuk understand that a world of chaos and suffering is not evidence that God isn't in control or doesn't care:

"Look at the nations and watch—and be utterly amazed. For I am going to do something in your days that you would not believe, even if you were told. I am raising up the Babylonians, that ruthless and impetuous people, who sweep across the whole earth to seize dwellings not their own."

Habakkuk 1:5–6

God is telling Habakkuk that the Babylonians—a sinful, militaristic, pagan nation—will be used as unwitting instruments in his hand to bring about judgment against the Israelites for their idolatry. God has not abandoned justice; his justice is at work, even if it is in ways that Habakkuk might not understand or appreciate. In verse 12, we see Habakkuk's reply:

Lord, are you not from everlasting? My God, my Holy One, you will never die. You, Lord, have appointed them to execute judgment; you, my Rock, have ordained them to punish. Your eyes are too pure to look on evil; you cannot tolerate wrongdoing. Why then do you tolerate the treacherous? Why are you silent while the wicked swallow up those more righteous than themselves?

Habakkuk 1:12–13

- What do you make of Habakkuk's reply?
- In what ways does he affirm God's character?
- Does God's reply entirely satisfy Habakkuk's complaints?

The presence of evil, pain, and injustice in our world does not mean that God isn't there or does not care. We live in a world that is warped by sin, and we experience the consequences of that. Throughout the Psalms, we see the ancient Israelite writers simultaneously affirming two things that don't seem to go together—the difficulties of a painful life, and God's goodness. We must follow their example and be willing to hold those two ideas up at the same time: Life can be hard and God can be good. Psalm 13 illustrates this concept in only six verses:

> How long, Lord? Will you forget me forever? How long will you hide your face from me? How long must I wrestle with my thoughts and day after day have sorrow in my heart? How long will my enemy triumph over me? Look on me and answer, Lord my God. Give light to my eyes, or I will sleep in death, and my enemy will say, "I have overcome him," and my foes will rejoice when I fall. But I trust in your unfailing love; my heart rejoices in your salvation. I will sing the Lord's praise, for he has been good to me.
>
> Psalm 13:1–6

- What stands out to you about these verses?
- Have you ever cried out to God in this way?
- What characteristics of God do these verses affirm?

Perhaps the most famous psalm in the Bible is Psalm 23, which paints a beautiful picture of God's presence in our lives and concern for us during dark times. It is written from the perspective of a sheep, who looks to God as a loving, attentive shepherd. Notice again the theme that God is with us and loves us even in the rough seasons of life. The psalm does not promise that there won't be dark valleys in life; it promises that God is *with us* in the dark valleys.

> The Lord is my shepherd, I lack nothing. He makes me lie down in green pastures, he leads me beside quiet waters, he refreshes my soul. He guides me along the right paths for his name's sake. Even though I walk through the darkest valley, I will fear no evil, for you are with me; your rod and your staff, they comfort me.
>
> Psalm 23:1–4

- What stands out to you about these verses?
- What do you think it means to view ourselves as a sheep?
- If God is the shepherd in this psalm, how would you describe God?

God loves us and is with us even when life is hard. And he sympathizes with us. He does not feel concern for us in some theoretical, detached way. Jesus cares for us in the up-close way described in Psalm 23 because he is the shepherd. As Jesus said,

> "I am the good shepherd; I know my sheep and my sheep know me—just as the Father knows me and I know the Father—and I lay down my life for the sheep."
>
> John 10:14–15

Because Jesus took on flesh and walked the earth as we do, he really does understand what it's like. He experienced pain and loss and rejection. As the writer of Hebrews put it:

> We do not have a high priest who is unable to empathize with our weaknesses, but we have one who has been tempted in every way, just as we are—yet he did not sin. Let us then approach God's throne of grace with confidence, so that we may receive mercy and find grace to help us in our time of need.
>
> Hebrews 4:15–16

Summary

Question: Where is God when I suffer?

Answer: He is with you in the dark valley. He knows how it feels, he knows your heart, and he loves you.

Leader tip: When people in your group are going through a hard time, remind them that God loves them, is walking with them through the dark valley, and really does understand how it feels. Encourage them to pray not for God to be close (because he is), but for an increased awareness of God's presence and that they would trust him.

Prayer

1. Starting with yourself, ask the group for two things:
   - A quick update on any ongoing prayer requests
   - New prayer requests
2. Write down the prayer requests as people share:

3. Ask someone in the group to close your meeting with prayer.
   - **Sample prayer:** Dear Lord, it's comforting to know that you understand how it feels to go through hard times. I believe that you, my Good Shepherd, are with me in the dark valleys, and I pray that you would help me to trust that. Help me to feel your presence when I'm struggling. Help me to have the courage to turn *toward* you when things are going wrong. Holy Spirit, help me to not turn away from

you when I struggle. I want to experience your presence and comfort. Amen.

4. In the next day or so, send a message to your group with the specific prayer requests so that you can be praying for each other between now and the next meeting.

14

How Can I Repair Broken Relationships?

Social

A few questions to get your gathering started. This can be done during a meal or at the outset of your meeting.

- **Personal question:** Give us a quick snapshot of how things have been going since our last meeting—maybe a high and low point. (Everyone answers.)
- **Open-ended spiritual question:** What's something you feel God is teaching you right now? (A couple people share.)
- **Lead-in question to the subject of the study:** Have you ever experienced true, lasting reconciliation with someone after a deep hurt, and if so, how would you describe the experience?

Study

Christians are not immune to broken relationships. Just as knowing and following Jesus does not guarantee us a comfortable life, we are not promised relational harmony when we place our faith in Christ. In fact, when you read the New Testament letters, they are full of teaching material that relates to conflict, which tells us that there were many broken relationships in the early Church. The first-century Christians fought about all kinds of things, including theology, morality, personal relationships, cultural engagement, and how to manage the affairs of local congregations. Jesus's teachings, too, assumed that his followers would experience conflict on a regular basis. This is why he spoke so often about forgiveness.

As we addressed in an earlier session, Jesus called us to be peacemakers, which means he knew that we would not be at peace with each other and would need to be proactive about seeking it out. As Jesus said in Matthew,

> "Blessed are the peacemakers, for they will be called children of God."
>
> Matthew 5:9

If we are peacemakers, we will be exhibiting one of God's family traits. This means that when we find ourselves in a broken relationship, we should not be okay with it. We should be willing to do the prayerful, emotionally laborious work of peacemaking.

- Assuming we all want peace in our relationships, why is peacemaking so hard?

Reconciliation is at the heart of the gospel. Jesus came to earth in order to pave the way for us to be reconciled to him.

He came to repair that vertical relationship between humanity and himself. But he also set an example for us so that we would experience horizontal reconciliation—the healing of broken relationships with other people in our lives. The apostle Paul spoke about this:

> If anyone is in Christ, the new creation has come: The old has gone, the new is here! All this is from God, who reconciled us to himself through Christ and gave us the ministry of reconciliation: that God was reconciling the world to himself in Christ, not counting people's sins against them. And he has committed to us the message of reconciliation. We are therefore Christ's ambassadors, as though God were making his appeal through us.
>
> 2 Corinthians 5:17–20

- How might reconciliation be viewed as a ministry, as Paul puts it?
- How does it change your view of relationships to know that God has committed to you a message of reconciliation?
- What do you make of the last phrase, "as though God were making his appeal through us"? What's the relationship between reconciliation in Jesus's name and God making an appeal through us?

Reconciliation, therefore, is not something that happens easily or automatically; it must be deliberately desired and doggedly pursued. We must view ourselves as recipients of God's reconciling effort in Christ so that we can then—as his ambassadors—become agents of reconciliation toward others in our own lives and communities. This is not easy, because there are many personal, social, and cultural boundaries that effortlessly cause conflict.

In the first century, one of those boundaries was the division between Jews and Gentiles. There were Christians from a Jewish background, and Christians from a Gentile (i.e., non-Jewish) background. Despite deep differences in their cultural, linguistic, and religious backgrounds, Jewish and Gentile Christians were meant to live in unity under the banner of Christ within the Church. Easier said than done. In his letter to the Christians in Ephesus (who were mostly Gentile), Paul helped them to understand that because of Christ, the religious and cultural boundaries that used to separate them no longer had any power to divide because of the cross:

> Remember that formerly you who are Gentiles by birth and called "uncircumcised" by those who call themselves "the circumcision" (which is done in the body by human hands)— remember that at that time you were separate from Christ, excluded from citizenship in Israel and foreigners to the covenants of the promise, without hope and without God in the world. But now in Christ Jesus you who once were far away have been brought near by the blood of Christ.
>
> For he himself is our peace, who has made the two groups one and has destroyed the barrier, the dividing wall of hostility, by setting aside in his flesh the law with its commands and regulations. His purpose was to create in himself one new humanity out of the two, thus making peace, and in one body to reconcile both of them to God through the cross, by which he put to death their hostility. He came and preached peace to you who were far away and peace to those who were near. For through him we both have access to the Father by one Spirit.
>
> Consequently, you are no longer foreigners and strangers, but fellow citizens with God's people and also members of

his household, built on the foundation of the apostles and prophets, with Christ Jesus himself as the chief cornerstone. In him the whole building is joined together and rises to become a holy temple in the Lord. And in him you too are being built together to become a dwelling in which God lives by his Spirit.

Ephesians 2:11–22

- What stood out to you about this passage?
- What words/concepts did Paul use to describe the relationship between Jews and Gentiles before Christ, and what words/concepts did he use to characterize them in light of what Jesus did?
- What person or group in your life do you feel is on the other side of a "dividing wall of hostility"? How can you build bridges to them?
- What hope does this passage offer to people who are experiencing relational brokenness?

In Paul's perhaps most overlooked letter, Philemon, he wrote to make peace between a Christian slave owner (Philemon) and his runaway slave, Onesimus, who became a Christian through Paul's influence after fleeing. In the brutal first-century Roman world, which viewed slaves as subhuman and routinely executed fugitive slaves, it is hard to imagine a more broken relationship than the one between Philemon and Onesimus. Yet Paul applies the gospel to this situation and encourages peace and a new perspective. He writes to Philemon:

Although in Christ I could be bold and order you to do what you ought to do, yet I prefer to appeal to you on the basis of love. It is as none other than Paul—an old man and now also a prisoner of Christ Jesus—that I appeal to you for my son

Onesimus, who became my son while I was in chains. Formerly he was useless to you, but now he has become useful both to you and to me.

I am sending him—who is my very heart—back to you. I would have liked to keep him with me so that he could take your place in helping me while I am in chains for the gospel. But I did not want to do anything without your consent, so that any favor you do would not seem forced but would be voluntary. Perhaps the reason he was separated from you for a little while was that you might have him back forever—no longer as a slave, but better than a slave, as a dear brother. He is very dear to me but even dearer to you, both as a fellow man and as a brother in the Lord.

So if you consider me a partner, welcome him as you would welcome me.

Philemon 1:8–17

- How does Paul describe Onesimus, the runaway slave?
- How would you describe the tone Paul uses in the letter as he addresses Philemon?
- What new perspective does Paul hope to impart to Philemon?
- In what ways does Paul's approach in this passage inspire you as you think about reconciliation and peacemaking?

Now that we have some sense of what biblical reconciliation is all about, we must ask an important question: How do we do this? In theory, we all want to heal broken relationships in our lives, but when we're hurt, it becomes very difficult to find our way toward peace. We might fumble our way toward a ceasefire, but true reconciliation often evades us. The reason for this is that we try to achieve reconciliation in our own strength, as if it's simply a matter of swallowing our pride, trying to forget about an offense, or begrudgingly saying the right words.

If we try to reconcile with others in our own strength, the peace will be superficial, unstable, and possibly even self-serving. To be ambassadors of reconciliation, as Paul put it, to be the peacemakers that Jesus described, we must rely on the Holy Spirit to work through us. We cannot manufacture Christlike reconciliation on our own. When Jesus went to the cross, he did not minimize our sins or pretend that they were not offenses; it was *because* they were so serious that he intervened with his life. If we are to reconcile with others in a way that even faintly resembles what Jesus did for us, we have to rely on him to work through us. Mercifully, the Spirit does just that.

In Galatians, Paul speaks about the fruit of the Spirit and lists qualities that are outward signs of the Spirit's inward work. We are not meant to work hard to achieve these character traits; they are the inevitable outgrowth of the Spirit's work in our lives. That is why they are called fruit. These qualities prepare us for a life marked by peacemaking and reconciliation:

> The fruit of the Spirit is love, joy, peace, forbearance, kindness, goodness, faithfulness, gentleness and self-control. Against such things there is no law. Those who belong to Christ Jesus have crucified the flesh with its passions and desires. Since we live by the Spirit, let us keep in step with the Spirit. Let us not become conceited, provoking and envying each other.
>
> Galatians 5:22–26

- Which of the fruit of the Spirit have you seen at work in your own life?
- Which do you feel are the most important for peacemaking?

Summary

Question: How can I repair broken relationships?

Answer: Relying on the Holy Spirit, embrace the role of peace-maker because of what Jesus did for you on the cross.

Leader tip: When you hear group members being unwilling to reconcile with others or not knowing how or why they should, remind them that they need to view their role as peacemaker as an outgrowth of what God did to make peace with them. They need to rely on the Holy Spirit for this to be possible; they can't reconcile with others in their own strength.

Prayer

1. Starting with yourself, ask the group for two things:
   - A quick update on any ongoing prayer requests
   - New prayer requests
2. Write down the prayer requests as people share:

3. Ask someone in the group to close your meeting with prayer.
   - **Sample prayer:** Heavenly Father, I want to be a peace-maker and an ambassador of reconciliation, but I

admit that I typically become blinded by my own pride and sense of hurt. Help me to do what you did, Jesus: take seriously the ways I have been hurt while simultaneously looking for ways to build bridges and reconcile. I cannot do this on my own—I need your help. Thank you for your love, and for your work to reconcile with me. Amen.

4. In the next day or so, send a message to your group with the specific prayer requests so that you can be praying for each other between now and the next meeting.

15

How Should I View My Money and Possessions?

Social

A few questions to get your gathering started. This can be done during a meal or at the outset of your meeting.

- **Personal question:** Give us a quick snapshot of how things have been going since our last meeting—maybe a high and low point. (Everyone answers.)
- **Open-ended spiritual question:** What's something you feel God is teaching you right now? (A couple people share.)
- **Lead-in question to the subject of the study:** What has been your relationship with money throughout your life? What do you wish it would be?

Study

God wants us to live a rich life, but not the kind of rich life we might imagine for ourselves. He wants us to experience the riches of his love, grace, and presence, and he desires that we find rest as we trust in him and look forward to the unimaginable joys of eternal life.

If there is one thing in our lives that has the most power to distract us from the rich life God wants for us, it is money—and the status and security we think it provides. This is why Jesus spoke so often about money and possessions; they will rule us if we let them. Whether we are wealthy or poor, money—or the desire for it—can subjugate our hearts.

But God gives us a road map for financial freedom, and it's not mainly about managing our money well. The road to financial freedom—from God's perspective—is about trust and generosity. As we acknowledge that God has given us everything we have, we trust him by giving some of it away for his purposes. Our generosity shows that we trust God, and it helps us continue to place our trust in him instead of in our possessions.

Behind all the biblical teachings about money is the concept of stewardship. Simply put, our stuff is not our stuff. Our money, possessions—and even other intangible resources like time, intelligence, and opportunities—are all given to us by God to be used for his purposes. We are not owners of what God has given to us; we are stewards, or managers, of it.

- What do you think about this concept of stewardship? How does it compare with the cultural view toward possessions and the accumulation of wealth?

In the biblical world, most people's resources were tied to land and livestock. Money was used, of course, but it was not as widely circulated or relied upon as it is in the twenty-first century. This being the case, it should not surprise us that when money is spoken about in the Bible, it is discussed against the backdrop of a mainly rural, agricultural context. So we read about fields, harvests, fruit, and wine instead of bank accounts and credit cards. But the underlying principles of trust, generosity, and stewardship are the same.

In the Old Testament, we encounter several important concepts that should shape our view of our own money and possessions. In this session we will address three: tithing, gleaning, and firstfruits.

Tithing

The tithe in ancient Israel was one-tenth of one's income set aside for the Lord's purposes. God was very clear with this command:

> "'A tithe of everything from the land, whether grain from the soil or fruit from the trees, belongs to the Lord; it is holy to the Lord.'"
>
> Leviticus 27:30

- What do you think it means that the tithe belongs to the Lord and that it is holy?

In Deuteronomy, we discover some of God's reasons for the tithe:

> Be sure to set aside a tenth of all that your fields produce each year. Eat the tithe of your grain, new wine and olive oil, and the firstborn of your herds and flocks in the presence of the Lord your God at the place he will choose as a dwelling for his Name, so that you may learn to revere the Lord your God always. But if that place is too distant and you have been blessed by the Lord your God and cannot carry your tithe (because

the place where the Lord will choose to put his Name is so far away), then exchange your tithe for silver, and take the silver with you and go to the place the Lord your God will choose. Use the silver to buy whatever you like: cattle, sheep, wine or other fermented drink, or anything you wish. Then you and your household shall eat there in the presence of the Lord your God and rejoice. And do not neglect the Levites living in your towns, for they have no allotment or inheritance of their own.

At the end of every three years, bring all the tithes of that year's produce and store it in your towns, so that the Levites (who have no allotment or inheritance of their own) and the foreigners, the fatherless and the widows who live in your towns may come and eat and be satisfied, and so that the Lord your God may bless you in all the work of your hands.

Deuteronomy 14:22–29

- What are some of the reasons given for the tithe? Why do you think this is important?
- One of the purposes of the tithe was to shape the heart of the giver: "so that you may learn to revere the Lord your God always." How do you think tithing leads to reverence?

The tithe, therefore, was a clear-cut standard set out by God, designed to provide for the ministry of the priests and those in need, but also to cultivate obedience and reverence in the hearts of the Israelites. It was not a strictly pragmatic rule; it was also a mechanism of spiritual growth, to make sure that the people were not ruled by their possessions. As we'll see, all of God's commands about money ultimately point back to our hearts. He cares for us and does not want to see us enslaved to our money or the pursuit of it.

Gleaning

In addition to the regular, planned tithe, God commanded his people to manage their crops in a particular way, that is, to be deliberately careless when they harvested their fields so that there would be some leftovers. This was an additional mechanism to spur generosity above and beyond the tithe. As it says in Leviticus,

> "'When you reap the harvest of your land, do not reap to the very edges of your field or gather the gleanings of your harvest. Do not go over your vineyard a second time or pick up the grapes that have fallen. Leave them for the poor and the foreigner. I am the Lord your God.'"
>
> Leviticus 19:9–10

- What is the reason for the practice of gleaning?

In effect, God was asking the Israelites to live below their means. They were commanded to tithe, and then to not even keep the entirety of the remaining 90 percent so that the poor would be provided for.

- What would be a modern approach to the gleaning principle? How could you implement this thinking in your life?

In Deuteronomy, God gives additional reasons for his commands related to gleaning:

When you are harvesting in your field and you overlook a sheaf, do not go back to get it. Leave it for the foreigner, the fatherless and the widow, so that the Lord your God may bless you in all the work of your hands. When you beat the olives from your trees, do not go over the branches a second time. Leave what remains for the foreigner, the fatherless and the widow. When you harvest the grapes in your vineyard, do not go over the vines again. Leave what remains for the foreigner, the fatherless and the widow. Remember that you were slaves in Egypt. That is why I command you to do this.

Deuteronomy 24:19–22

God was telling the Israelites that they should take care of the vulnerable because he had taken care of them when he rescued them from Egypt. Once again, it goes back to the heart. If we understand how much God has given to us, it will propel us toward generosity. We will plan for structured giving (the tithe) as well as leaving room in the budget for sporadic giving as needs present themselves.

Firstfruits

When you have entered the land the Lord your God is giving you as an inheritance and have taken possession of it and settled in it, take some of the firstfruits of all that you produce from the soil of the land the Lord your God is giving you and put them in a basket. Then go to the place the Lord your God will choose as a dwelling for his Name and say to the priest in office at the time, "I declare today to the Lord your God that I have come to the land the Lord swore to our ancestors to give us." The priest shall take the basket from your hands and set it down in front of the altar of the Lord your God.

Deuteronomy 26:1–4

To give of the firstfruits was an act of trust. It was to offer to the Lord a portion of your harvest before you have harvested everything. It is preemptive, sacrificial giving—offering to the Lord his portion first, rather than allocating leftovers to him.

Tithing, gleaning, and the offering of firstfruits helped to shape the hearts of God's people. They had to plan to give, be ready to give spontaneously, and be prepared to give preemptively before even knowing what their total harvest would be.

- How can we embrace a firstfruits mentality toward our income today?

Anyone who followed Jesus around would have heard him speak often about wealth and its many pitfalls. In perhaps the most famous words he spoke about money, he lays it out very clearly:

> "Do not store up for yourselves treasures on earth, where moths and vermin destroy, and where thieves break in and steal. But store up for yourselves treasures in heaven, where moths and vermin do not destroy, and where thieves do not break in and steal. For where your treasure is, there your heart will be also. . . . No one can serve two masters. Either you will hate the one and love the other, or you will be devoted to the one and despise the other. You cannot serve both God and money."
>
> Matthew 6:19–21, 24

- What stands out to you about these verses?

Here again we see the emphasis on the heart. If our heart is given over to our possessions, it significantly hinders our relationship with God. In this next passage, the parable of the rich fool, Jesus speaks about the dangers of placing our trust in our possessions:

Someone in the crowd said to him, "Teacher, tell my brother to divide the inheritance with me."

Jesus replied, "Man, who appointed me a judge or an arbiter between you?" Then he said to them, "Watch out! Be on your guard against all kinds of greed; life does not consist in an abundance of possessions."

And he told them this parable: "The ground of a certain rich man yielded an abundant harvest. He thought to himself, 'What shall I do? I have no place to store my crops.'

"Then he said, 'This is what I'll do. I will tear down my barns and build bigger ones, and there I will store my surplus grain. And I'll say to myself, "You have plenty of grain laid up for many years. Take life easy; eat, drink and be merry.""'

"But God said to him, 'You fool! This very night your life will be demanded from you. Then who will get what you have prepared for yourself?'

"This is how it will be with whoever stores up things for themselves but is not rich toward God."

Luke 12:13–21

Based on these verses, you might think the parable is mainly about hubris—being foolishly confident in one's wealth. In a superficial sense, it is about that. But there's a deeper meaning, explained by Jesus in the very next verses:

Then Jesus said to his disciples: "Therefore I tell you, do not worry about your life, what you will eat; or about your body, what you will wear. For life is more than food, and the body more than clothes. Consider the ravens: They do not sow or reap, they have no storeroom or barn; yet God feeds them. And how much more valuable you are than birds! Who of you by worrying can add a single hour to your life? Since you cannot do this very little thing, why do you worry about the rest? . . .

"Do not be afraid, little flock, for your Father has been pleased to give you the kingdom. Sell your possessions and give to the poor. Provide purses for yourselves that will not wear out, a treasure in heaven that will never fail, where no thief comes near and no moth destroys. For where your treasure is, there your heart will be also."

Luke 12:22–26, 32–34

Jesus has revealed that worry is behind much of our attitude toward money. Our anxiety about the future and our security leads us to give our hearts to our money rather than to God. Our trust is in our possessions instead of him.

- What has been the relationship of money and worry in your life? Do they go hand in hand?
- Why do you think that worrying is so hard to leave behind?
- If you had to summarize Jesus's teachings about money that we have read in this session, how would you characterize them?

Let's close this session with some words of the apostle Paul to his protégé Timothy. His comments tie together several themes we have covered in this session:

Command those who are rich in this present world not to be arrogant nor to put their hope in wealth, which is so uncertain, but to put their hope in God, who richly provides us with everything for our enjoyment. Command them to do good, to be rich in good deeds, and to be generous and willing to share. In this way they will lay up treasure for themselves as a firm foundation for the coming age, so that they may take hold of the life that is truly life.

1 Timothy 6:17–19

Wealth is so uncertain. Our hope is in God. The truly rich life is about trusting in him and being generous. Living that way will allow us to lay up treasure in heaven—to deepen our relationship with God—so that we can live a life that is *truly* life.

Summary

Question: How should I view my money and possessions?

Answer: As God's resources, entrusted to you so that you can manage them according to his purposes. Our money is not our source of security or hope; God is.

Leader tip: If the subject of money comes up in your group, do your best to remind your group members that it is a heart issue. All of God's commands about money are ultimately to help us deepen our relationship with him and live out his purposes. He wants to spare us enslavement to our money, which cannot—and will not—deliver in providing us hope or security.

Prayer

1. Starting with yourself, ask the group for two things:
   - A quick update on any ongoing prayer requests
   - New prayer requests

2. Write down the prayer requests as people share:

3. Ask someone in the group to close your meeting with prayer.
   - **Sample prayer:** Lord, I want to honor you in the area of my possessions. I want to be generous and trust in you. I do not want to be captive to worry or search for security in earthly objects. I want to give my whole heart to you, and I acknowledge that my possessions and pursuit of money are great obstacles. Help me, Lord. I trust you. Amen.
4. In the next day or so, send a message to your group with the specific prayer requests so that you can be praying for each other between now and the next meeting.

16

What Should I Think about People Who Don't Share My Beliefs?

Social

A few questions to get your gathering started. This can be done during a meal or at the outset of your meeting.

- **Personal question:** Give us a quick snapshot of how things have been going since our last meeting—maybe a high and low point. (Everyone answers.)
- **Open-ended spiritual question:** What's something you feel God is teaching you right now? (A couple people share.)
- **Lead-in question to the subject of the study:** How do you typically feel about people who don't believe what you do, especially when it comes to spiritual matters?

Study

As a result of our sinful nature, we humans are prone to division. We notice differences in others, and instead of appreciating them or looking for the good, we are often offended, threatened, or just plain annoyed by the differences we see. Broken relationships, wars, political bickering, racism, sexism, arguing online—it feels like we are bombarded continuously with opportunities to view others with contempt.

Technology, generally speaking, has not helped. Social media and the twenty-four-hour news cycle have further splintered our culture by highlighting the differences and divisions between us.

The Church is not immune to these realities. We Christians live in the same world, with the same pitfalls and temptations. And we face potential conflicts on two fronts: within the Church and between the Church and the rest of the culture. In a culture that seems to prefer division and conflict, we Christians must discover an appetite for unity and peace. We must do this even with people who think very different things than we do, whether it's brothers and sisters in Christ with differing theological views, or people who do not share our faith or worldview. This is our clear call, as we will see in this session.

- What are some of the divisions you see within the Church, and how might they be remedied?
- How would you characterize the relationship between the Church and the rest of the culture? What can we Christians do better to align our hearts and minds with Christ?

Jesus gave us some very helpful and memorable metaphors for how Christians should think about people who don't believe what they do. In the gospel of Matthew, Jesus said we are to be salt and light:

> "You are the salt of the earth. But if the salt loses its saltiness, how can it be made salty again? It is no longer good for anything, except to be thrown out and trampled underfoot. You are the light of the world. A town built on a hill cannot be hidden. Neither do people light a lamp and put it under a bowl. Instead they put it on its stand, and it gives light to everyone in the house. In the same way, let your light shine before others, that they may see your good deeds and glorify your Father in heaven."
>
> Matthew 5:13–16

- Salt brings out flavor and acts as a preservative. What does it look like for Christians to be the salt in a society?
- Light is beautiful and drives out darkness. It exposes the truth and gives hope. In what way(s) can Christians be light in our culture?
- How does being conflict-prone hinder our ability to be salt and light?

Another concept—a lens—that Jesus gave us was that of an ambassador. We are called to be ambassadors of Jesus to a watching and hurting world. Diplomats don't invent the message they bring; they represent the one who has sent the message. In our case, that's Christ. Look at how Paul describes the nature of our ambassadorship:

> Therefore, if anyone is in Christ, the new creation has come: The old has gone, the new is here! All this is from God, who reconciled us to himself through Christ and gave us the

ministry of reconciliation: that God was reconciling the world to himself in Christ, not counting people's sins against them. And he has committed to us the message of reconciliation. We are therefore Christ's ambassadors, as though God were making his appeal through us. We implore you on Christ's behalf: Be reconciled to God. God made him who had no sin to be sin for us, so that in him we might become the righteousness of God.

2 Corinthians 5:17–21

- According to Paul, what sort of ambassadors are we meant to be?
- How does the gospel shape the way we represent Jesus?
- What do you think it means to be ambassadors of reconciliation to people who don't believe what we do?

We are salt and light in the world, and we serve as Christ's ambassadors. These ideas speak to our words, actions, tone, and motives, and they are contrary to an argumentative, condemning attitude that comes so easily to many of us.

Jesus's disciple Peter, when he wrote a letter to some Christians who were struggling, spoke about how we should interact with others, especially those who don't believe what we do. As you read these verses, take note of what you find personally encouraging or challenging.

Finally, all of you, be like-minded, be sympathetic, love one another, be compassionate and humble. Do not repay evil with evil or insult with insult. On the contrary, repay evil with blessing, because to this you were called so that you may inherit a blessing. For, "Whoever would love life and see good days must keep their tongue from evil and their lips from deceitful speech. They must turn from evil and do good; they must seek peace and pursue it. For the eyes of the Lord are on the righteous and his ears are attentive to their prayer, but the face of the Lord is against those who do evil."

Who is going to harm you if you are eager to do good? But even if you should suffer for what is right, you are blessed. "Do not fear their threats; do not be frightened." But in your hearts revere Christ as Lord. Always be prepared to give an answer to everyone who asks you to give the reason for the hope that you have. But do this with gentleness and respect, keeping a clear conscience, so that those who speak maliciously against your good behavior in Christ may be ashamed of their slander.

1 Peter 3:8–16

- What stood out to you about these verses? Which qualities are hardest for you to embrace?
- What does it mean to seek peace and pursue it?
- What does it look like to be prepared to give your reasons for the hope you have in Christ?
- How can we as Christians embrace a gentler and more respectful approach to talking with others about our faith, as Peter encouraged us to do?

The apostle Paul set a wonderful example for us in this area. He reached out to people of all backgrounds—people who believed very different things than he did and were even antagonistic to his message. He was adaptive and just kept sharing the gospel. He did not view antipathy as a sign that he shouldn't speak about Christ. In Acts 17, we get a glimpse of how creative and determined Paul was to engage with people who did not (yet) share his worldview.

While Paul was waiting for them in Athens, he was greatly distressed to see that the city was full of idols. So he reasoned in the synagogue with both Jews and God-fearing Greeks, as well as in the marketplace day by day with those who happened to be there.

Acts 17:16–17

Paul spoke with Jews in their own houses of worship, and he spoke to Greeks who had converted to Judaism. He also spoke in the business community with whoever happened to be there. Most of the people he encountered would have had very different views on God, but Paul did not view himself as being their adversary; he viewed them as someone who needed Jesus. Paul would be baffled by the culture-war mentality that so many Christians embrace today.

Let's look at one final passage in this session, perhaps the one that speaks most clearly to the question of how we should view those who don't share our worldview.

Be wise in the way you act toward outsiders; make the most of every opportunity. Let your conversation be always full of grace, seasoned with salt, so that you may know how to answer everyone.

Colossians 4:5–6

- What is the main quality Paul suggests we have when talking to those who don't believe what we believe?
- We should speak with grace, and our words should be seasoned with salt. What do you think he means by these two qualities?

Summary

Question: What should I think about people who don't share my beliefs?

Answer: View them as people whom God loves just as much as he loves you, and people to whom he has sent you as his ambassador to share the good news of Jesus Christ with gentleness and respect.

Leader tip: When members of your small group speak with scorn about people who are not Christians, remind them that we are not meant to despise nonbelievers; we are meant to love them and share Christ with them as his ambassador.

Prayer

1. Starting with yourself, ask the group for two things:
   - A quick update on any ongoing prayer requests
   - New prayer requests
2. Write down the prayer requests as people share:

3. Ask someone in the group to close your meeting with prayer.

- **Sample prayer:** Lord Jesus, it is hard for me to think rightly about those who don't believe what I believe. I confess that I judge them and have a condemning attitude toward them. I admit that I don't seek out opportunities to share the gospel as much as I should, and when I do, my words haven't been as gentle and respectful as they could have been. I need you, Holy Spirit, to shape my heart and my words so that I can interact with others as Jesus's ambassador. I trust you to help me in this area. Amen.

4. In the next day or so, send a message to your group with the specific prayer requests so that you can be praying for each other between now and the next meeting.

17

What If I Have Doubts about God or Something the Bible Says?

Social

A few questions to get your gathering started. This can be done during a meal or at the outset of your meeting.

- **Personal question:** Give us a quick snapshot of how things have been going since our last meeting—maybe a high and low point. (Everyone answers.)
- **Open-ended spiritual question:** What's something you feel God is teaching you right now? (A couple people share.)
- **Lead-in question to the subject of the study:** When you have doubts or questions about something the Bible says, what do you do to find answers? How have your questions been received when you've asked someone?

Study

I am convinced that one of the great misunderstandings of the Christian faith is that we must never have any serious questions. Questioning God or the validity of the Bible is a sign of a weak faith, many believe. This is not true. Scripture is full of people who doubted God, wrestled with the truth, got frustrated at God's actions (or inaction), and asked the Lord hard questions.

We must never forget that the God of history stepped into his own creation at a particular moment in time. Jesus took on flesh to fulfill his rescue mission, and in the process, God became observable like never before. Jesus's ministry was public. He knew people. He had friends. Jesus's ministry was witnessed by thousands of people, and the documents about Jesus's life and the early Church (the New Testament) were written down very soon after the events they described, during the lifetimes of people who knew Jesus.

As the writer of Hebrews put it:

> In the past God spoke to our ancestors through the prophets at many times and in various ways, but in these last days he has spoken to us by his Son, whom he appointed heir of all things, and through whom also he made the universe. The Son is the radiance of God's glory and the exact representation of his being, sustaining all things by his powerful word.
>
> Hebrews 1:1–3

God spoke to us by his Son, who was the exact representation of God. This tells us that God acted in a manner to deliberately make himself known to us. He invites us to know him—to know who he is and to seek out clarity about his nature and purposes. A God who loves us and goes so far out of his way to make himself known is not rattled by our questions and doubts.

- What do you think about the Hebrews text above?
- How does it shape your view of Jesus's mission?

In 1 Corinthians 15, Paul cites what many scholars believe to be an early statement of faith (or creed). He says, "What I received I passed on to you," and then he goes into a section that seems to summarize the basics of what first-century Christians believed happened with Jesus:

> Now, brothers and sisters, I want to remind you of the gospel I preached to you, which you received and on which you have taken your stand. By this gospel you are saved, if you hold firmly to the word I preached to you. Otherwise, you have believed in vain. For what I received I passed on to you as of first importance: that Christ died for our sins according to the Scriptures, that he was buried, that he was raised on the third day according to the Scriptures, and that he appeared to Cephas, and then to the Twelve. After that, he appeared to more than five hundred of the brothers and sisters at the same time, most of whom are still living, though some have fallen asleep. Then he appeared to James, then to all the apostles, and last of all he appeared to me also, as to one abnormally born.
>
> 1 Corinthians 15:1–8

- What does this statement of faith describe about Jesus?
- What is the significance of listing eyewitnesses to these events?

When the message of Christianity was first making its way into Europe, Paul and his friends came to a town in Greece called Berea. Paul and company had run into some opposition on their journey, but they encountered something remarkable at Berea— people who were eager to learn and ask the hard questions.

As soon as it was night, the believers sent Paul and Silas away to Berea. On arriving there, they went to the Jewish synagogue. Now the Berean Jews were of more noble character than those in Thessalonica, for they received the message with great eagerness and examined the Scriptures every day to see if what Paul said was true. As a result, many of them believed, as did also a number of prominent Greek women and many Greek men.

Acts 17:10–12

- What stood out to you about the Bereans as Luke describes them?
- How does this text relate to our question, "What if I have doubts about God or something the Bible says?"
- How can we follow the example of the Bereans?

God, therefore, made himself known and observable in Jesus's life, and he made sure that there were plenty of eyewitnesses around and lots of evidence for posterity to know what happened. We saw with the Bereans, too, that asking the hard questions about faith is a good thing.

But even with solid reasons for believing what we do about God, this does not guarantee a vibrant faith or growing relationship with the Lord. For example, just after Jesus did a very large-scale, public miracle (the feeding of the five thousand), some of his followers balked at his teaching and stopped following him:

Jesus said to them, "Very truly I tell you, unless you eat the flesh of the Son of Man and drink his blood, you have no life in you. Whoever eats my flesh and drinks my blood has eternal life, and I will raise them up at the last day. For my flesh is real food and my blood is real drink. Whoever eats my flesh and drinks my blood remains in me, and I in them. Just as the living Father sent me and I live because of the Father, so the one who feeds on me will live because of me. This is the bread that came down from heaven. Your ancestors ate manna and died, but whoever feeds on this bread will live forever." He said this while teaching in the synagogue in Capernaum.

On hearing it, many of his disciples said, "This is a hard teaching. Who can accept it?"

Aware that his disciples were grumbling about this, Jesus said to them, "Does this offend you? Then what if you see the Son of Man ascend to where he was before! The Spirit gives life; the flesh counts for nothing. The words I have spoken to you—they are full of the Spirit and life. Yet there are some of you who do not believe." For Jesus had known from the beginning which of them did not believe and who would betray him. He went on to say, "This is why I told you that no one can come to me unless the Father has enabled them."

From this time many of his disciples turned back and no longer followed him.

John 6:53–66

Similarly, Jesus's disciple Thomas would not believe Jesus was raised from the dead unless he could empirically observe Jesus's body alive again. And Jesus had something very surprising to say to Thomas after he allowed him to do just that:

Now Thomas (also known as Didymus), one of the Twelve, was not with the disciples when Jesus came. So the other disciples told him, "We have seen the Lord!"

But he said to them, "Unless I see the nail marks in his hands and put my finger where the nails were, and put my hand into his side, I will not believe."

A week later his disciples were in the house again, and Thomas was with them. Though the doors were locked, Jesus came and stood among them and said, "Peace be with you!" Then he said to Thomas, "Put your finger here; see my hands. Reach out your hand and put it into my side. Stop doubting and believe."

Thomas said to him, "My Lord and my God!"

Then Jesus told him, "Because you have seen me, you have believed; blessed are those who have not seen and yet have believed."

John 20:24–29

- What stood out to you about these two passages?
- Why do you think Jesus suggested it would have been better for Thomas to have believed without seeing? Wasn't Jesus's appearance to them partly about proving his resurrection was real?

God invites our questions and gives us good reasons to believe in him, but that does not mean that empirical evidence will lead us to a question-less faith in God. Faith will always be part of the equation. But it is a reasonable faith, based on plenty of historical evidence.

If you're looking for a specific answer to a question about the Bible, here are a few suggestions to make sure you're getting good information from reliable sources:

1. Contact your pastor.
2. Consult a study Bible.
3. Contact a seminary or Christian college professor.
4. Buy a book that is published by a reputable Christian publisher.

On one final note, remember that Jesus calls us to himself—to seek him, to ask the hard questions, to wrestle with the deep matters of faith. He is not annoyed or intimidated by our questions. He wants our whole hearts and minds. In Matthew 7, we read one of his invitations:

> "Ask and it will be given to you; seek and you will find; knock and the door will be opened to you. For everyone who asks receives; the one who seeks finds; and to the one who knocks, the door will be opened."
>
> Matthew 7:7–8

We are invited to knock on the door, and he is waiting to welcome us in. But if we read a little further in the New Testament, we also see that when we knock on the door, he has been knocking on the other side:

> Here I am! I stand at the door and knock. If anyone hears my voice and opens the door, I will come in and eat with that person, and they with me.
>
> Revelation 3:20

The point is this: When we seek Jesus with our whole hearts—tough questions and all—we find that he hasn't just been waiting for us; he's been seeking us, too.

Summary

Question: What if I have doubts about God or something the Bible says?

Answer: Ask the hard questions but also seek the true answers. God made himself observable for a reason, and he invites us to seek him.

Leader tip: When people in your group seem reluctant to ask hard, honest questions about God, encourage them to fully explore their questions and seek answers.

Prayer

1. Starting with yourself, ask the group for two things:
   - A quick update on any ongoing prayer requests
   - New prayer requests
2. Write down the prayer requests as people share:

3. Ask someone in the group to close your meeting with prayer.
   - **Sample prayer:** Lord Jesus, I know that you came to earth to be known and to rescue us. I admit that I have deep questions that sometimes scare me a little bit. I sometimes struggle to find the answers, but I trust you. Please help me to find the answers to my questions. Encourage me, Holy Spirit, as I seek to know you better. Help my questions and doubts not to make me worried or anxious; help me to view them as opportunities to grow. Amen.
4. In the next day or so, send a message to your group with the specific prayer requests so that you can be praying for each other between now and the next meeting.

Conclusion

Some Reassurances about Leading a Small Group

We've covered a lot of ground together. We have explored the various practical, emotional, and spiritual challenges that are inherent to small-group leadership, and we have considered some of the most common and consequential questions of our faith. We have also discovered the unique opportunities and deep joys that are only found in gatherings of Christians that are small.

In closing, I will briefly restate some of the key ideas we covered in parts 1 and 2 of this book. My hope is that this review will not only reinforce what you've learned, but also that it would provide a final, concentrated dose of reassurance as you step into this historic and worthwhile endeavor of small-group leadership.

Part 1: Practical Starting Points

- If you choose to lead a small group today, you have stepped onto a well-worn path, a time-honored tradition of the Church.

- God has worked powerfully through the millions of men and women who have led groups over the centuries, and you can rest assured that he will work through you as well.
- There is no one-size-fits-all approach for leadership.
- A small group might be effective at nurturing spiritual growth at the cost of your enjoyment as the leader. If this is the case, you will eventually exhaust yourself and the group's effectiveness will suffer. Make sure you are enjoying your own group!
- Asking the right questions—not having all the answers—will set the stage for growing friendships and a deeper engagement with God's Word.
- Leading a small group is a biblical, God-honoring thing to do.
- Keep a watch on your expectations; transformation takes time, and it's God's business.
- Rely on the Lord and keep meeting.
- Satan—the accuser and tireless cynic—wants you to think that you're not up to the task of leading. He wants you to effortlessly remember your flaws and dwell on your supposed shortcomings. Don't be surprised when he lies to you about your group and your leadership.
- The antidote to your inner critic isn't about trying harder, learning more, or being better. It's about asking Jesus to replace your earthly definitions of leadership with his.
- Leading others in a small group is not about your competence or knowledge or proving your worth. It's about serving and relying on Jesus to do his work through you.
- Be your group members' friend, a facilitator of meaningful conversations, and an example to your group— not a model of perfection, but an example of someone

who is faithfully following Christ and trusting him through the ups and downs of life.

- It is wise to know the challenges that will probably arise with leading a small group, and to preemptively manage both the problems themselves and your expectations about them.
- No small group will ever have perfect attendance, and holding yourself as a leader to that standard—or anything close to perfect attendance—is an unrealistic expectation that will only discourage you.
- Each group is unique.
- You as the leader are the constant. Just keep meeting and be happy to see whoever shows up.
- God might use your leadership and encouragement to raise up a new leader who will go on to make a lasting impact on others for many years.
- If you get the impression that you've offended someone or you sense a relational distance between you and someone in your group, go directly to that person and speak privately about it.
- Gentleness is the operative word when confronting troublesome group members.
- Embrace the awkward silences!
- Try to make your own contributions to the group discussions a follow-up to someone else's comment.
- Don't view the discussions as opportunities for you to speak; view them mainly as opportunities to listen.
- If you overprepare for your group discussions, you will exhaust yourself in the long run and rob yourself of the joy of experiencing the study in real time with your group members.

- Let your group members see you wrestling with the material alongside of them—asking honest questions and wondering about how to personally apply the biblical text.
- People *will* ask questions you did not expect and questions you don't know how to answer.
- Your goal is not to present yourself as some omnicompetent persona, but rather to set an example.
- Show your group what it looks like to turn toward Jesus—the Good Shepherd—in the dark valleys of life. Let them see you lead imperfectly. Let your guard down and ask for their prayers and help.
- Jesus is both your example and your source of strength as you lead, and that's a comforting thought.

Part 2: Starter Small-Group Studies

- **What is God like?** Look to Jesus and find out.
- **What is grace?** God's gift of undeserved favor.
- **How does God view me?** You resemble him. You're worth dying for. In Christ you're a new creation. In Christ you are God's child.
- **What does it mean to have faith in God?** To trust him because he is God and he is trustworthy.
- **How do I grow spiritually?** Make choices that align with God's commands, trusting that the Holy Spirit is the one who is transforming you and enabling you to live a God-honoring life.
- **What is sin and how does it affect my life?** Sin is a rebellion against God. It is a condition and also choices that we make. If we are in Christ, then we have been set free from sin's dominion, though we do still sin sometimes.

- **How should I pray?** Honestly and consistently, with the main goal being a deeper relationship with God.
- **Where is God when I suffer?** He is with you in the dark valley. He knows how it feels, he knows your heart, and he loves you.
- **How can I repair broken relationships?** Relying on the Holy Spirit, embrace the role of peacemaker because of what Jesus did for you on the cross.
- **How should I view my money and possessions?** As God's resources, entrusted to you so that you can manage them according to his purposes. Our money is not our source of security or hope; God is.
- **What should I think about people who don't share my beliefs?** View them as people whom God loves just as much as he loves you, and people to whom he has sent you as his ambassador to share the good news of Jesus Christ with gentleness and respect.
- **What if I have doubts about God or something the Bible says?** Ask the hard questions but also seek the true answers. God made himself observable for a reason, and he invites us to seek him.

As you go forward from here as a small-group leader, I leave you with these encouraging words from the book of Hebrews:

May the God of peace, who through the blood of the eternal covenant brought back from the dead our Lord Jesus, that great Shepherd of the sheep, equip you with everything good for doing his will, and may he work in us what is pleasing to him, through Jesus Christ, to whom be glory for ever and ever. Amen.

Hebrews 13:20–21

Ryan Lokkesmoe is the lead pastor of Real Hope Community Church in the Houston area. As an undergrad, he studied criminal justice before going on to earn his MA in New Testament at Gordon-Conwell Theological Seminary and his PhD in New Testament at the University of Denver. His doctoral work focused on the historical context of first-century Christianity.

Ryan previously served as the small-groups pastor of a large multisite church, personally consulted with ministry leaders from around the country about small groups, and developed small-group curriculum for LifeWay. Ryan is the author of *Blurry: Bringing Clarity to the Bible* and *Paul and His Team: What the Early Church Can Teach Us about Leadership and Influence* and also teaches biblical studies at a local seminary.

Ryan loves music and books and is both a history buff and a close follower of current events. But most of all, he loves spending time with his wife and their two children.